INTELLIGENT SEARCH

Finding the best talent for your company and the best company for your talent

By

Pamela Ciccantelli

ISBN: 1-4033-2295-3 (ebook)
ISBN: 1-4033-2296-1 (Paperback)

Library of Congress Control Number: 2002091477

This book is printed on acid free paper.

Printed in the United States of America
Bloomington, IN

1stBooks - rev. 10/29/02

Dedicated to the 100+ recruiters with whom I've had the pleasure of working over the course of my career along with the hundreds of truly inspiring team members at ISCG. I learned so much from all of you as we pushed the limits of our hellishly exhilarating roller coaster ride. Many thanks for all the fun.

Contents

Part 1: Company Search

Introduction

For as long as there's been commerce and industry, it's been important to attract and retain the best talent, but with the modern shift from manufacturing to the new "information economy," staffing has become *the* key competitive difference between corporate winners and losers. To put it into the parlance of today's business world, staffing is now a core competency. While most companies will admit that hiring the sharpest available candidates is their key challenge in today's world, very few of them have studied what makes a successful hiring team or for that matter know how their own company's staffing model works—or in many cases, doesn't work.

We are all familiar with the expression "Give a man a fish and he eats for a day. Teach him to fish and he eats for a lifetime." This book is meant to help companies hire more effectively and educate job seekers so they are better able to conduct a successful job search. Our intention is a simple one. It is to teach companies how to compete for employees and individuals how to compete for jobs, so you are no longer dependent on outside services. These pages compress fifteen years of recruiting experience, with an emphasis in the technical world, into as few pages as possible. It includes my insights from having been a professional recruiter—*headhunter* if you prefer—for many years. Having completed multiple retained searches, having built an effective internal recruiting team for a technical consulting company, and having acted as a consultant to organizations regarding their internal recruiting functions have all contributed to the knowledge base of this book.

Intelligent Search is written to be a quick read and offer a common sense look at the hiring process from the perspective of both the company and the candidate. It is geared to companies hiring into areas that require professional skills, whatever those skills may be. It will answer questions that every professional recruiter has been asked repeatedly in our careers. It will address some basic points that are missed by both companies and candidates in their search for each other. In the short term it can provide some easy-to-implement guidelines. In the long run, it can make a significant difference in how to conduct our own searches as companies or as individuals, and potentially make or break our fortunes.

Chapter 1, Conducting an Intelligent Search

Recruiting is a funny business. While there is nothing technically complex about hiring people, there is very definitely a method and talent to hiring the right people. If you picked up this book and are beginning with *Part I, Company Search*, you are most likely someone who works in a hiring capacity in your company. Like most hiring managers, you are also probably frustrated from time to time with the lack of effectiveness of your own hiring methods. Although few companies would claim that they hire successfully and in a timely fashion every time, unfortunately, there are many companies for whom hiring is more like a roll of the dice than a precise business process. Why is that? Someone just starting out in the recruiting business once asked me, "How hard can it be? You call, schedule, interview, and make an offer." Sounds pretty simple, right? Then why do so many people complain about how poorly it works in their companies? These complaints vary but generally they include "It takes too long to fill a position," "the cost of hiring is too high," "dissatisfaction with the eventual hire," or "lack of retention after a long drawn out search." What causes these fairly common complaints?

The first answer is that while most people believe hiring should be simple, in reality, most of them do not do it for a living. It is a secondary, or even tertiary responsibility to the other duties involved in their position. While some of these managers have excellent business judgment, they lack the instinctive hiring judgment that can only be developed through experience and through a career whose primary responsibility is interviewing and hiring. It is this experience that makes a professional recruiter just that—a professional. Unless you have interviewed hundreds or thousands of candidates every year for many years, you haven't experienced enough successes and failures to have a solid hiring track record. To assume that any person can be as successful as any recruiter, is to assume that any recruiter can do the job of any manager.

A common reason that companies are less successful at hiring than they'd like to be is that very few managers want to admit that they do not have the required skills. For some strange reason, recruiting, interviewing and hiring is something everyone assumes they know how to do even before they've ever done it. They feel insulted at the suggestion that they may not innately know what to do. This is unfortunate because while it is almost impossible to teach the instincts that come from years of recruiting, most managers can be taught some key steps for successful interviewing if they are receptive to advice. Ask any hiring manager if they were ever given a class on what to look for in an interview *before* they ever interviewed and very few of them will say yes beyond being told basic legal regulations.

Along with these causes is the clear fact that recruiting has changed significantly over the years. It is no longer a question of finding resumes. Companies have more resume sources than ever and in most cases have resume databases that contain thousands of resumes. Recruiting has become a matter of how well those resumes are used, screened, interviewed, treated, and eventually *invited into* an organization.

An Intelligent Search means using a better strategy and process for attracting and retaining employees. It begins with an admission that we are not doing this very well. At the very least, we are not doing it as well as we would like. It requires an open ear and a willingness to absorb the ideas that career recruiters learn over time. It also requires a clear understanding of your own company, the hiring practices

5

being used, and the short- and long-term goals of your company beyond filling any one specific position. The most effective course of action will vary depending on those goals. While most companies will say that hiring the right talent is critical to their company success, most of them regard their recruiting process much like the scene in the Wizard of Oz where they are told "Pay no attention to that man behind the curtain." Recruiting is somewhat of a mystery to them.

Let's begin with a detailed example. Consider Company A, a large, bureaucratic Fortune 500. They are a fully developed, multinational company with over 50 years of business success. This success can breed a complacency that business will continue as usual whether or not the position gets filled in a timely way. While it may be an inconvenience to others on the staff to leave this position empty, the company stock price does not plummet because of the inefficiency. Company B, on the other hand, is a small business, perhaps a dot-com startup. This company may fail or succeed based on how well and how quickly they move to find the right person. Filling a position in Company B has an entirely different sense of urgency. That open position can cost the company a significant amount of revenue. However, Company B is also in a different financial situation and is less likely to be able to spend an undetermined amount of money on filling the position and is restricted by their available funds. How these two companies hire are probably very different. How these two companies hire *should* be very different.

Looking more closely at these examples, let's review how they are probably structured and the reality of each situation. Company A, the large corporate conglomerate, most likely does nothing to fill this position until they have a position description that details the position level to whom it reports, grade of the position, salary range, position title, and all of the position responsibilities. This description may have been defined by the hiring manager or by a representative of the Human Resources (HR) department. While this is a critical component to success, the time involved in putting this description together may be days or even weeks. Until this step is completed, no efforts are made to begin a search.

In Company B, this loss of time would be unacceptable. In Company B, there are fewer people involved in the job definition. It may be clear or vague, but guaranteed, it is not yet in writing anywhere. Ever. Company B has a good idea of what they need but will verbally communicate those instructions without ever setting them in writing. Company B often does not have defined salary ranges, position titles, or for that matter, any idea of more than some of the responsibilities that will be expected of this new position. Small companies and start-ups need candidates who are willing and able to wear as many hats as possible.

Is one more right than the other? Not necessarily. Each situation requires its own process. Company A, while they will describe the position as needing to be filled "yesterday," has the luxury of time that Company B simply does not have. This drives two very different behaviors each with its own challenges.

What does Company A do next? Probably they will run an ad and post the position internally. Running an ad may take another week or two depending on when the ad agency is able to whip something together and when the newspaper deadline is for the next classified ad. Posting the position internally and possibly adding it to the company web site may or may not happen but if so, could take up to a couple of weeks to submit. Depending on how progressive Company A is with their recruiting methods, they may or may not post to an Internet site. It has now been a month or more since they determined this was a new position. As of yet, no candidate's resumes have been reviewed for consideration. In many of these companies even the internal processes are unwieldy so the department that needs the position filled may never know if another department already interviewed the perfect candidate. There is no efficient process for passing that candidate to another department.

What did Company B do? In most cases, someone picked up the phone and immediately called a few agencies and described the position. As long as the salary ranges and qualifications were realistic, the agencies were able to send over some resumes within a matter of hours or days and interviews were scheduled within the week. While Company B may have moved more quickly and have more visible results, they will also spend unnecessary dollars for agency fees. Both companies must be aware of how much they are willing to spend to fill a position but also bear in mind the cost of not filling a position in a timely way.

A final consideration that both companies must address is whether this is a position that will need to be filled many times over the course of the year or is a one time hiring need. For example, Company A may need multiple administrative hires throughout the year and multiple computer programmers but only need to hire a business strategist once in five years. Company B, while much smaller, will also have roles in the organization that have similar responsibilities that are needed several times in the same year. When positions must be filled multiple times each year, having a standard position description that only needs to be adapted can be a real time saver.

Another issue involved in conducting an Intelligent Search is the level of the position within the organization. While any hiring mistakes are a headache, at more senior levels within an organization, the damage that can be done and the visibility of the error are much greater, so it becomes more critical that the hire be successful. The tactics for filling very senior level talent versus a junior one should be different.

Our next chapters will cover these basic considerations and outline the steps that are most cost effective and efficient in filling any position.

Chapter 2, Creating Requirements Definitions

As any recruiter will tell you, one of the most frustrating situations occurs when hours are spent tracking down the right candidate, interviewing them, and presenting them to hiring managers, only to find that the requirements changed or were never clearly defined at the outset. Defining a position is not just about what is ideally required but also about what can be dropped from the requirement if it becomes impossible to find the ideal. In other words, where are the parameters rigid and where can they be stretched?

Most experienced recruiters are huge fans of the stretch hire. The benefits are felt mutually by the candidate and the company. For the new hire there is the advantage of coming into a situation that offers an immediate learning challenge. To the talented contributor, this makes the position that much more appealing especially if the skills to be learned will benefit their future careers. For the hiring company, they've immediately widened the pool of great candidates and opened the door to the possibility of getting a very able worker for less salary than one with those skills. Managers who are very good at stretch hiring tend to take a lot of pride in watching their hires grow professionally. The realization that they were able to provide an opportunity for someone overlooked by less astute hiring managers has a definite reward. Very often, it also breeds an unshakable loyalty from the employee. Here's one recruiter's words about the stretch hire:

> *"When I'm looking for a candidate, at first I outline everything I would hope to find in any one person. Then I accept the fact that I've probably*

*just created an unrealistic profile. So I ask myself
which piece can they learn and which pieces do I
absolutely need from the get-go. If I start a search
for a candidate and five months later I still have
no one on board, I could easily have spent the
first two or three months sending him to training
on at least one or two of the supposed position
requirements."*

This basic rule of thumb—when to use stretch—is one
of the key components of an Intelligent Search.
Overlooking it is also one of the most common mistakes
that companies make in their searches. In the quest for the
perfect candidate, the hiring manager passes on several
viable candidates because they are missing one or two
pieces of the puzzle. While the importance of a position
definition cannot be overemphasized, it is equally important
to realize that getting 100% of a description is unlikely.
Decide right from the start that certain qualifications may be
less important and which are a necessity.

Many companies will define the position requirements
thinking of every single component that the job may require
of them. Usually the position description is based on the
profile of the last person to hold that role and sometimes it
is *even written* by that person. What a manager fails to
remember is that the person exiting the job may have had
only half those skills when they first started. The rest they
learned as they gained experience in the role and through
training that was provided over the years. They literally
grew into the role and now the manager expects the next
hire to walk in having all the pieces from day one.
Repeatedly over my own recruiting career I've heard
managers say "Get me somebody else like Mark" and I need
to remind them that they didn't want Mark when they first
interviewed him and needed to be persuaded to hire him,
but within a few months he became a top performer.

Let's take a look at an example of a position description that will never be filled:

> *We are seeking a technical professional with an absolute minimum four years experience in systems and application development utilizing C/C++. This candidate must have a BSCS, strong programming languages, and knowledge of Linux and AIX. Experience with object-oriented design, communication protocols, embedded systems and device drivers is required. Point-of-sale, bank networks and experience in control appliances is a must.*

The only possible explanation for why someone would write a job description like this one is because they already have the candidate in mind and are writing it to fit his experience. Otherwise the description limits the candidate pool so extensively that it will never be filled. Everything is a must or an absolutely required. Would this company pass on someone who had all of the above but only three years of experience? What if they had everything but point-of-sale experience? These may still be highly qualified candidates based on what they bring to the table on day one. Understanding what elements of a position are expendable is as important as knowing which are not. The person is more likely to exist if the position description reads as follows:

> *We are seeking a technical professional with experience in systems and application development utilizing C/C++. This candidate should have a BSCS or comparable work experience, strong programming languages, and knowledge of some form of a Unix-based system. Experience with object-oriented design is*

> *required. Development involving communication protocols, embedded systems and device drivers is preferred. Point-of-sale, bank networks, and experience in control appliances is a plus.*

Now the description allows for what is required, namely real world experience with C/C++. They can also stretch to any flavor of Unix. This will require somewhat of a learning curve but not an impossible stretch for anyone who fits the rest of the description. The type of development work would ideally be in some area of communication protocols or device drivers and anything in the actual application area would be strongly in their favor. This significantly opens the pool of potential candidates letting the hiring decision makers make stronger judgment calls on stretch candidates.

In the definition phase of the candidate search, ask yourself "What will this person be doing their first month on the job?" Whatever that primary responsibility will be should dictate the required portion of the definition. For example, in hiring an administrative assistant, someone with no computer skills is not going to be able to do even the first day on the job without training. But the administrative assistant who has computer skills but has never used a particular software package can probably walk right in and be productive with a little assistance. If they are smart, they can take the manual home or work a few extra hours each evening until they are up to speed. Or they can be sent to a quick training course in their first month and be as accomplished as the candidate coming in with that particular skill.

It's important to remember that in most cases this is not a life or death decision. Unless of course, you are hiring brain surgeons in which case, the exact experience is critical. I would, however, add a word of caution regarding the stretch hire when it comes to senior executive level positions. At senior levels within any organization, I advise against the stretch hire. Take for example a VP of sales. This VP has very specific goals. I may expect him to double the sales organization and increase revenues by 25%. When I consider a candidate for this role, I want to see that exact experience within the same industry. This is not the time to take a chance on someone who has never done it but believes they can and wants the opportunity to try. There is simply too much at stake for the company. But at all other levels the stretch can be the difference between an OK hire and a great hire.

So why are so few companies willing to take a chance? Most often it is a lack of confidence in their personal judgment. This same lack of confidence is the reason that so many companies try to include as many people as possible in the interview process. If for whatever reason the new hire doesn't work out, it seems to reflect less poorly on those in the interview process if they can justify it by saying, "She had every qualification we needed." Taking responsibility for a poor hire is never easy but it is a fact of life that we are all fooled from time to time. In my observations I've noticed that the more hiring a manager does the more likely they are to take calculated risks. The more they make successful calls and gain trust in their own judgment, the less likely they are to be overly cautious about the consequences.

I have seen very few exceptions to this rule but from time to time I've met managers who simply never improve. My advice to them is to get someone else to do the hiring— really. We all have one friend, who no matter how hard they try, just can't pick the right friends or spouses. It's as though they have a blind spot when it comes to good sense about people. It would be in their best interest to eventually accept that this is a weakness and rely heavily on the advice of their friends in choosing a lifelong partner. I suggest that hiring managers with poor track records do the same.

The stretch rule also applies when it comes to salary negotiation, a topic we will explore at length later in the book. Consider this scenario:

> *"We had been interviewing candidates for over two months and we found one candidate that we all felt really good about but what he was asking in compensation was outside our salary guidelines. I later found out that the candidate took a job in another part of the company for less than he had discussed with me because they offered him some alternatives like an extra week of vacation and a minor sign-on bonus. I could have kicked myself for not having made an offer and negotiated these points with him."*

When it comes to the salary that a company is willing to pay a candidate, it is important to establish clearly in your own mind the exact drop-dead-can't-get-around-it number. Only by knowing the exact number, rather than fixating on the broad range, can you be sure you're going as far as you can on salary. If you meet a candidate stronger than the one described can the position level be elevated? Are there sign-on bonuses, extra vacation, or other perks that are going to help negotiate the eventual offer? Much like buying a home or a car, we all need to have an idea of what we can afford. However, sometimes we miss a great buy that only needs a little work to exceed our expectations. On the other hand, knowing that even the house of our dreams isn't affordable at a certain price, helps us set a ceiling on what we will explore.

Chapter 3, The Options for Finding Candidates

So now you have your position carefully defined and you are anxious to start seeing resumes and candidates. The next step depends in large part on where the responsibility lies for filling the position. This varies greatly one organization to the next. In the majority of large corporations, the main responsibility falls in the Human Resource department. Most of these HR departments are overworked with their limited resources stretched over an area that includes not just recruiting but also compensation issues, employee relations, legal and naturalization considerations, EEO requirements, and more. In a structure such as this one, there is generally speaking no one in Human Resources who came from a straight recruiting background. By this I do not mean to imply that they haven't had a great deal of interviewing experience in their backgrounds. What I do mean is that they were never trained as a recruiter or made a living with recruiting being the only focus of their responsibilities. In other organizations there is a separate department dedicated to recruiting. In still others, the individual hiring manager takes on the responsibility and becomes the focal point for all of the recruiting activities.

Since each method of starting a search will be explored more fully in subsequent chapters, let me first give my own preferred order of a search irrespective of your own organization's structure. What is the number one way to start the pipeline of candidates flowing? Answer: employee referrals. Someone once said everything we need to know, we already know. In the world of recruiting this tends to be another rule of an Intelligent Search. In most cases, someone in your organization can probably refer a qualified candidate given the proper incentive and motivators. Simply put, *your own co-workers are your best source of potential candidates*. Statistically a referred prospect is much more receptive to the interview and offer than someone who knows nothing about your company. Hires brought in through an Employee Referral Program (ERP) are also more likely to acclimate and stay longer than any other source of hire. We'll cover the topic of ERPs in full detail in Chapter 5, so let's continue with the order of preference for other ways to attract candidates, and deal with each in more depth in future chapters.

After employee referrals, the next most important option is to *post the position on the Internet job sites* with which you have been most successful in the past. This will be the topic of Chapter 4, and one that requires more cost concern than the first course of action.

Following employee referrals and Internet sites, which are easily the top two sources for resumes, it becomes more of a level playing field depending on your locale and how much money you have to spend in the hiring process. Why does the region matter? In some metropolitan areas newspapers and local media, including radio and TV, are still viable options for attracting candidates to your company. However, in many parts of the country, the newspaper classifieds are dwindling rapidly as anyone can measure based on your local paper and whether that section has grown or shrunk in the past five years. Local radio and TV media have at best, a splotchy success story, and we will explore why in Chapter 6.

The type of hiring and how many openings you will have also impact which steps to take in filling positions. *Job fairs and open houses* can be a great source of potential candidates but require significant planning and media advertising to be successful and will be costly and time consuming. However, these are still very positive sources of both company visibility and candidate prospects. Another source of candidates especially in times of significant downturn are any local outplacement services. These services do not charge any fees and provide access to their database of candidates that have been recently let go from local and national corporations. These three considerations will all be addressed more fully in Chapter 6.

Another much overlooked source of candidates is the company's own *database of resumes*. In the early 1990's, many companies did not have an organized system for collecting, holding, and searching resumes. However, by the late 90's it became the norm for companies to have some type of repository that could be used effectively given you have enough manpower to pursue this source. If every resume ever received is somehow tracked, even in its most rudimentary form, that resume database becomes a goldmine of potential candidates. Today it is not unusual for such a database to have tens of thousands of resumes. How accessible those resumes are to various search criteria is another matter. Choosing the appropriate resume database for your company needs could be the subject of a book in itself.

At this point, if you've reviewed all of these sources for resumes and candidates and none fit your current organization's resources, there is always the option of turning the entire affair over to an outside service that will handle the candidate search for you. It may offend most professionals in these services, both contingent and retained, to be considered a last option, but the purpose of this book is to teach companies to become independent of the need to rely so heavily on outside services and create a more structured internal approach to attracting candidates. Every company has at their disposal multiple options and in conducting an Intelligent Search, it is critical that these options are each explored.

To summarize, here are the options for finding candidates, in the order they should be considered:

1. Employee referrals

2. Internet job sites

3. Company resume
   Database

4. Job fairs

5. Open houses

6. Outplacement services

7. Local print and media

8. Outside services,
   contingent or retained

After seeing our list of options, perhaps you're asking "Why is no mention made of the company website?" While your own website is a great source of candidates and should certainly have a section leading prospective employees to the proper person within the organization, the website itself is rarely responsible for making candidates aware of your company. Instead, some other source generally causes the candidate to seek out the website.

The statistics on hiring through a website are currently skewed beyond any meaning because it doesn't push the issue of "Why did you go to that company website?" Did you see an advertisement and decide to explore further? Was the advertisement for an upcoming job fair or open house? Did a friend recently join that company and speak well of the experience? Did the company respond to an Internet site posted resume and the candidate was drawn to the website when they received some sort of notification from the company? These are all questions that must be effectively answered since candidates rarely pull a company name out of thin air and decide to find the website except in the case of large corporations with maximum name recognition. So the company website is definitely a great magnet for pulling in resumes and a cost-effective way to post current openings, but it cannot be considered a source to attract candidates until companies look deeper than the initial contact.

One more insufficiency of collecting resumes from your website is that very often they require the candidate to submit information in cut and paste format. These resumes are very difficult to read when pulled from your website. Until this feature improves, it may be more practical to allow the reader to send his already formatted word document to a specific web address such as jobs@xyzcorp.com. Not only does this make it easier for the candidate but also much easier for anyone trying to read the resume in a legible format.

Chapter 4, The Increasing Role of Internet Research

One of my strongest suggestions as we head into the 21st century is to get yourself a topnotch, experienced Internet researcher (IR) to support your recruiting efforts. I was extremely fortunate in my recruiting career for many reasons, but one of the blessings I value most is that my company hired a very capable Internet researcher to support the recruiting team. At the time all seven recruiters, myself included, were skeptical and resistant to the idea that any of us needed the help of someone to do our research for us. The arguments ran something like this, "Any good recruiter can do their own research on the Internet and should be Internet-fluent." Even today, none of us would disagree with that statement. However, my own experience in watching the productivity and success of having one centralized Internet research group (one person became a team of four over the next three years) unanimously won our team over to the concept. An experienced Internet researcher lets your recruiters do what they should be doing—spending their time either on the phone or in an interview rather than surfing the web.

Why Internet research at all? Very simply, the Internet has the power to increase your recruiting productivity, shorten the hiring cycle, lower your cost per hire (even including the cost of the Internet researcher salary), and somewhat inexplicably, statistically improve your retention. One of my first concerns when we began heavily relying on the Internet and our Internet researcher was that those hires would be our highest source of turnover simply because it was easy for someone who was unhappy to post and jump any job situation—especially in the technical world where everyone spends their day in front of a computer providing easy access to the Internet job sites.

To my delight, my concerns proved unfounded. In the first two years of studying the statistics, the Internet went from our second lowest turnover source of hiring, to our source of lowest turnover hiring. We can all speculate on why this might be true but the numbers we ran in our hiring spoke for themselves. Maybe the person using the Internet to get a job has a chance to do a lot of shopping around and when they finally settle on a position are secure that it was the correct choice for them, thus opting to stay longer than they might under other circumstances. Maybe the Internet hire is more confident that they can conduct a relatively easy job search and tend to stick out a bad day or two at work knowing they can leave quickly should they finally make that decision. Whatever the reasons, the Internet is a strong asset in your recruiting efforts that cannot be denied and should not be neglected.

Whether or not your company does enough consistent hiring to require an Internet researcher is a decision each organization must judge for itself. My instincts say that even 20 hires a year warrants having an Internet researcher. It seems almost a necessity if hiring is over the 100 per year mark. Your Internet researcher should be dedicated to your recruiting or HR team but their skills can also be used as an Internet Market Researcher during hiring slow times.

Regardless of whether you bring in an Internet researcher, the use of the Internet is a required tool if your company does significant hiring of computer professionals each year. Technical professionals are heading more and more towards the Internet as their first line of defense in a job change. My own forecast is that within another three years or so, the technical portion of the classifieds will be almost non-existent as that portion of the population relies more and more heavily on Internet posting. Judging by major metropolitan newspapers around the country, the technical segment of the population is consistent in their direction towards the Internet.

However, there are many portions of the population still a step or two away from using the Internet as a way to change jobs. I say a "step or two" intentionally implying that within 10 years it will be an accepted norm for most non-technical job seekers as well. While an administrative assistant or a healthcare provider may not consider going that route, I can envision within a year or two, having services that do that leg of their job search for them, still providing the benefit without requiring the technical savvy. In more rural areas of the country this may take a little longer to take root but there is no doubt in my mind that eventually the Internet will replace newspaper classifieds and companies who missed the boat will be the worse off for not having taken advantage of Internet hiring benefits.

This notion of Internet hiring has some strong opponents. The arguments against Internet hiring from some senior level managers with whom I've worked leave me incredulous. One argument says, "Only a lazy job seeker uses the Internet. No one I want on my team would rely on it as a way to get a new position." The evidence is now overwhelming that such a perspective is simply dated. Internet job searching is most definitely here to stay and will grow dramatically in the next few years. Managers who flatly refuse to use the Internet will rapidly fall behind in the hiring game. Many of your positions will go unfilled for longer times due to your shortsightedness.

Once you understand the value of the Internet, the next question becomes "Which sites do we choose?" Good question as there are already countless sites around the country. Here again the value of having an Internet researcher comes into play. An experienced Internet researcher needs to closely monitor the success of your company hiring from various sites by taking advantage of the free trials that most sites initially offer. This monitoring will determine which sites are most effective for your particular type of hiring. Your researcher should be tracking not just how many resumes were pulled based on company postings but more importantly how many hires were made from each posting. They can also monitor how long it is taking for the candidate to get called after the resume has been passed to the responsible party. This will help analyze where the delay in getting a hire on board is happening.

There is no one site that is right for every company. Your first stop in evaluating job boards should be www.airsdirectory.com. This website offers a comprehensive listing of available sites. There are sites that are undeniably huge, Monster.com being way out in front right now. However, the licensing cost of Monster may prohibit many small to mid-size companies from using it and those costs are skyrocketing along with the success of that site. Keep in mind that while some of these costs appear prohibitive, much more than these amounts are spent each year on agency fees. Many of the sites including Monster will offer a one-time job posting for a month at a time that is very affordable—a few hundred dollars—and worth the cost especially if the type of skill advertised will be needed more than once over the course of a year. Additionally, there are dozens of other smaller but still powerful sites that can satisfy your needs. If all hiring is locally based, it may make sense to go with a job board that is locally-based and specializing in a particular industry. These tend to be much less expensive and still provide a significant source of successful hiring.

Job boards come in all shapes and sizes. There are simply too many to mention in this book. You can have boards that specialize in a particular industry such as pharmaceutical or healthcare, boards that specialize in international postings, ones that carry a heavier technical slant, ones that specialize in executive level positions such as 6figurejobs.com, and ones that specialize in independent contracting such as Dice.com. There are also sites that specialize in either work from home positions or ones that cover shorter workweeks or unusual work schedules. There are job sites for international positions, non-profit organizations, government, and women only. A very handy reference book to use is called "America's Top Internet Job Sites" by Ron and Caryl Krannich. The book is updated annually and available through most large book chains.

At the writing of this book, most sites have licensing fees that offer various packages. Most sites offer a variety of packages, such as specifying how many passwords or number of users per company along with how many postings are permitted each month. As mentioned, most will offer a free test period. They all have different search engine capabilities. The success of these search engines is one of the key measures that an Internet researcher will evaluate in reaching eventual decisions as to which sites to use. A good IR will measure not just how easy it is for the researcher to use but how easy it is for the candidate to use.

Throwing money indiscriminately at the Internet boards is as useless as throwing it away to outside services. Decisions regarding your Internet research activity must be made by someone who understands recruiting and ideally, by an experienced Internet researcher. As the value of this position becomes more obvious, the cost of these professionals will also increase but will be well worth that expense as it improves the hiring volume and shortens the hiring cycle. Companies spend a lot of time worrying about the cost of hiring and nowhere near enough time worrying about the loss of revenue when a position is not filled month after month.

One final word on the use of the Internet. An added bonus that can be gained from using the Internet daily is that it becomes a normal course of business to find many of your own employees resumes on the system. Even when they block out their name it is relatively easy to spot when someone in your organization has posted a resume on a job site. This gives any employer the opportunity to openly discuss that worker's frustrations and hopefully resolve the situation and avoid losing a good worker.

While each company really must look closely at how their own hiring breaks down on an annual basis to determine which sites are most helpful, the following list provides some sites that may be worth exploring just to get started. Once you've been using the Internet for even two years, the choice of sites should only be determined by proven, documented hiring success and bottom-line cost.

- Monster.com
- Dice.com
- HeadHunter.com
- JobCircle.com
- Minorities Job Bank
- ELance.com

- ComputerJobs.com
- JobBankUSA.com
- Net-Temps.com
- JobOptions.com
- careeraltavista.com
- 6figurejobs.com

Some pharmaceutical/healthcare related sites include:

- Jumping Pills.com
- Biospace.com
- ISPE.com

- DIA.com
- MiracleWorkers.com
- MedZilla.com

Some International Job Boards include:

- StepStone.com
- Fish4Jobs.com
- DatumEurope.com

- FirstTuesday.com
- Eurojobs.com
- Gisajob.com

Chapter 5, The Employee Referral Program

Employee referrals are your most valuable source of hiring, yet very misunderstood in many companies. Most companies consider the employee referral only as a way to fill a specific position within the organization. Employee referrals are so successful a tool, their use *must* be formalized into an Employee Referral Program (ERP) and insinuated into the entire business process and culture.

Every single employee within an organization brings with them a network that can be a huge source of hiring if it is correctly tapped. Let's say at its most conservative, each person who joins your company knows twelve people. Multiply that times the number of employees in your company and you've just built a very significant database of potential hires.

There are various reasons that companies do not take full advantage of this network that is right before their eyes. Problem number one is that *most companies do not broadcast their employee referral program effectively*. It is hidden away in the benefits book, usually buried in a late chapter and barely mentioned thereafter. The successful employee referral program must be promoted on a regular, monthly basis. It should be a top-down effort for which upper management takes responsibility. It must be talked about at meetings, conferences, and informal get-togethers. "Who do you know?" should be a question asked on a regular basis and *not* just by your Human Resources team. Everyone in the organization must understand that our company success is based on superior hiring practices and every co-worker is responsible for the company success.

Drawing attention to your ERP can be fun and exciting. If the payout to the employee is strictly monetary it should be a significant figure. It amazes me that companies that have no problem paying an agency they don't know $15,000 and up for a hire, somehow think that their own co-workers should be rewarded with a sum as small as $500. A successful ERP reward should be a minimum of $1000. Your program will start getting some serious attention when you're paying out $2500 and up. When hiring is at its most frenzied, $5000 should not be out of the question for tough-to-fill positions.

These higher amounts require close monitoring by whomever holds responsibility for the program and should not have strings attached to earning the reward. When it comes to an ERP, the simpler the better. It is important to be clear about the timeframe of the referral and the payout schedule for the reward. It is also important that your hiring team is keeping close tabs on when resumes have come in through various sources. If a resume is referred but has already been received through another source such as the Internet or a Job Fair, the referrer does not earn the bonus. However, should a referral come in the same day through two different sources it makes sense to honor the employee referral before other sources.

The ERP is a great motivator. It boosts morale and keeps your company one big happy family. The more people who join the firm who already know each other, the more likely they will stay with the company long enough to become significant contributors. As mentioned in Chapter 1, the acclimation and retention of referred employees is consistently higher than referrals through most other hiring sources.

Rewards for referrals don't always have to be cash. In fact, products and services offered as rewards can provide a great source of company visibility in your community—the more creative the better. For example, a company who built one of the most successful ERPs in which I had the privelege to participate, once had the entire community buzzing by offering a two-part reward. The first was a $5000 monetary payout for each hired referral. For part two, they put all ten names of the employees who successfully referred a new hire over a specific timeframe in a drawing; the winner was given a fully paid lease on a BMW for two years. Another drawing took the names of everyone who referred someone, regardless of whether they were hired, and the winner received five days/four nights in the Bahamas fully paid. The idea behind the drawings was to encourage those employees who made referrals who may not have gotten hired for whatever reason.

One huge mistake that companies make with their ERPs is expecting employees to qualify the person being referred. Many companies require that an employee referral match a particular job on your website. Your employees may know a lot of people but they are not talent scouts. The only qualification for a referral should be that your employee thinks highly of them. Leave the rest to the hiring team to make a decision on whether the referral is a fit and for which positions within the organization.

A successful ERP does not require that the person being referred be in an active job search. The goal should be to collect names and let your recruiters use those names as a source of calls. The call may say nothing more than "You were thought very highly of by someone who joined us recently and I wanted to give you the opportunity to learn more about us if you are ever in a job search. Are you interested at all in scheduling an appointment to learn more about our company?" This very simple call can lead to many prospective hires both short- and long-term.

Even the most successful and highly publicized ERP still needs personal prompting. To use the professional recruiter's term, it is a matter of constant "sourcing." Many times I can get names and contact info from someone who initially says, "I don't know anybody like that," by doing some personal sourcing. I may start with the obvious

29

prompts such as "Who impressed you where you used to work?" or "Who was the best manager in your career?" Eventually though I would branch out into "What about any relatives? Neighbors? People you know from the gym?" Without fail in the course of this one-on-one the light bulb goes on and I get a reply like, "Oh right! I forgot that one of the guys I play softball with is a salesperson!" Unless you are a recruiter, you probably overlook the most obvious potential referrals and so do your employees. The time that this takes is minimal but may still be beyond the means of most companies unless they have an internal recruiting team to perform this effort. An internal recruiting team can fill many such roles that the rest of the organization simply doesn't have time to do. This topic is discussed in detail in Chapter 8.

Beyond designing a successful employee referral program, the simple "Who do you Know?" question is your most likely source of executive level hiring. At senior levels, there is an even higher likelihood that someone knows the right person to fill that position. When a company goes to a retained search firm to fill a position, chances are the first thing they do is what your top management team could easily have done themselves. *They sit down and research who is your competition? Then they ask, within those organizations, who meets the responsibilities of your open position?* No one is more qualified to answer these questions than your own management team and nothing is more frustrating than paying a $50,000+ retainer to hire someone who is already a known member of your industry and familiar to your staff

One word of warning: It is still imperative that the person brought in as senior level talent not *just* be someone everyone knows. In the world of executive level hiring, there's little room for compromise regarding the track record of that candidate. They must have already successfully accomplished whatever it is that your company needs. They also must be knowledgeable with the business or services provided by your company. One of the more common mistakes companies make in hiring senior level executives is hiring an outstanding candidate, but one who has no experience having done what you need done.

If your own employees are reluctant to suggest their friends or former co-workers as referrals, a good question to ask yourself, is why? Do they have less than positive impressions of the organization? Are they unhappy in their current situation? Are they concerned about how this person's candidacy will be handled? Do they fear that the person referred will not get hired and that their personal relationship will be damaged? Most of these questions and issues can be answered and resolved by setting proper expectations. Let your employees know that not every person they refer will be called but each resume will be carefully reviewed for both current and future opportunities. Make it clear that they will be treated with utmost respect and then be sure that they do.

Now that we've covered two of the most successful sources of hires, the next chapter will highlight alternative sources of candidates including both mainstream and less visible sources.

Chapter 6, Other Hiring Sources

Newspaper "Help Wanted" Advertising: With the maturing of the Internet as a successful media for announcing open positions and posting resumes, there has been a proportional decline in the use of more traditional newspaper advertising as a hiring resource. This point will be hotly debated by many, especially those in the newspaper business, but I can only speak from my own observations as I travel the country comparing the metropolitan papers. What I've seen clearly shows a trend.

More specifically in many metropolitan areas, there is only one major paper to use for running a significant advertisement in the Sunday section. While there are several local suburban papers for running ads, those papers print during the week and carry less of an audience than the Sunday paper. Over the past 15 years, the size of classifieds have increased and decreased with most major newspapers. However, in the past three years the job classifieds have taken a marked dip in number of advertising pages. Hardest hit are sections that specialized in technical positions. At its height, this section saw mega issues with over 40 pages of job classifications, each company trying to capture the audience with larger and larger ads. It was not unusual to see more than one full page ad that easily cost those companies $30,000+ to run for one week.

As these technical job seekers turned more and more to the Internet, companies needed to allocate their budget accordingly and the newspaper classifieds became a less viable option based on cost. The cost of that one page, one week ad can buy a year long license on a job board like Monster allowing for hundreds of postings throughout the year. Whatever a company's budget, the cost savings in using the Internet can be tremendous. The point here is not that newspaper advertising is unwise—it will always serve a purpose. In a city with only one major newspaper there will always be a need for the job classified section. As mentioned earlier, there are also many fields unlike the technical field that have not yet transitioned into the Internet hiring model.

The reasons to run a print ad have changed over the years. While your company may want to run an ad to draw attention to a particular position, it is more likely that a certain number of ads should run each year *for the sake of company visibility*. Running an ad offers the opportunity for you to advertise your company and what it does. While we may all know what Campbell Soup does as a company, the majority of ads run in the classifieds are by companies that are less recognized in the marketplace. Running an ad tells your audience what types of jobs you have, where you are located, and offers the visibility that may attract any potential job seeker to your website. Once the potential job seeker has been drawn to your website, they are just a few clicks from being able to submit a resume.

Over the course of my recruiting career I've seen the number of resumes and hires made from print advertising drop significantly. While newspaper advertising initially counted for as much as 50% of hiring, it fell to a low that is now under 10% since the late 1990s. The good news is that using newspaper advertising as a visibility tool makes budgeting for print advertising much more predictable. By determining the number of ads to run each year it is much easier to stick to that budget.

In many areas the major paper works closely with organizations that run job fairs and in order to attend a particular job fair, your company is required to run a minimum size ad in the newspaper. If this is the case, deciding when to run ads is largely determined by job fair attendance. Let's take a closer look at what can and should be accomplished by local job fair attendance.

Job Fairs: Job fairs are a valuable ingredient of any company's hiring strategy. A job fair will quickly build your resume database, especially now that electronic copies of all resumes are provided. A job fair also gives those staffing the booth the face-to-face opportunity to gauge the "fit" of this person for your organization. In a quick five-minute exchange, you can save your company several hours of scheduled interviews. This is particularly advantageous in the case of candidates that look great on paper but do not present themselves as well as certain positions require. This information should be captured somewhere in your resume database to prevent any future time spent on this candidate. This may sound harsh to some, but the reality is that candidate presentation does not often change over the course of one's career. If for example, the service your company provides requires a high degree of communication skills for all positions, then any candidate unable to articulate their experience is not going to succeed in your interview process. I cannot over-emphasize the value of job fairs in making that assessment.

Job fairs are all run differently based on the company handling the logistics. Some are run right out of hotel suites allowing attendees from out of town the luxury of having somewhere to stay as well as interview. Other venues may include the local convention center or sports stadiums. I've seen no statistics that correlate success of a job fair with the venue but I've always felt some resistance towards conducting interviews in any room with a bed in it. It feels somehow inappropriate regardless of how successful the job fair may be. Some recruiters, however, are strong proponents of hotel suites because more private conversations are possible.

Job fairs are also another source of enhancing your company's image and a way for you to say to a wide audience, "Yes, we are hiring." In choosing which job fairs to attend, it helps to scout them out beforehand, by attending discreetly *as a job seeker*. This will give you the chance to see both audience and company attendance without spending what is generally a $2000+ entry fee. Once you've attended a few different job fairs, determining which to attend defaults to the usual metrics of "How many hires were made from each?" But again, do not neglect the value of having collected a significant number of resumes that may be suitable for future positions.

Job fairs must be manned with representatives who positively reflect your organization. While manning job fairs generally falls under the responsibility of HR or Recruiting, many companies use this opportunity by manning the booth with hiring managers. This provides hiring managers with a clear picture of available candidates and may educate them to reset their own hiring expectations in the future. Inviting a difficult manager who has been unhappy with HR's ability to provide candidates for a particular position to attend a job fair may provide a valuable lesson in candidate comparison.

Radio & Television Advertising: Many job fairs also offer radio and television advertising as a part of the job fair package. This opportunity to highlight your company name without carrying the usual cost of these relatively expensive forms of advertisement is another benefit of a job fair. The results of radio and television advertising are difficult to measure. Having sold recruitment advertising for a radio station at one point in my recruiting career, I had a chance examine how best to use these media. I became convinced that they are a very effective way to highlight a company event, but *not as successful as a standalone hiring campaign.* What this means is that if you want to reach an audience that is not job-seeking, and catch their attention for 30 seconds by putting your company name over the airwaves, *do not expect to see a measurable count of hires* based on the money spent. There are several intangible benefits such as boosting your own company morale, bringing name recognition—or in some cases, *name change* recognition—to an audience's attention. For these purposes radio and TV advertising may be well worth the money. If you have an upcoming company event that you want to publicize, such as an open house, then radio or television advertising can be very successful.

In choosing which stations to advertise, be sure to acquire and study the ratings for different stations and time slots. If your company population is heavily male oriented that is your first clue as to which stations to use. There are multiple services that track listener audience as the Nielsen ratings track television. You need to be careful as all radio stations are very good at skewing the numbers in the direction you want to see. None of them can say to you, "Most architects listen to WXYZ" or "Most computer professionals in your area listen to KLMN." They are however able to break down age, gender, and a few other population statistics but the surveys don't tend to go deep enough to be more specific. A good technique is to *poll your own employees*. Find out which two or three stations most of them listen to on their drive in and out of work and use those stations. Also be sure to look closely at time slots that your radio campaign is offering. While you need to have a few that run at odd hours of the day and night, a successful campaign requires that you also have a fair number of drive hours in order to maximize your listening audience.

Open Houses: The open house is yet another way to satisfy high volume hiring for your company. Your open house is actually a job fair with just your company in attendance. The term open house, however, usually implies that it is being conducted at your own company site. If your company accommodations are impressive, an open house can be a great way to show it off. Arranging a successful open house, however, takes a lot of work, money, and staff participation.

Once you've decided to run an open house be prepared to spend a minimum of $25,000. It is easy to spend $40,000 on a well-prepared open house with the majority of that money being spent on advertising including print, radio, and sometimes TV. Additional expenses will include refreshments for attendees, handout materials, and promotional giveaways. An open house must present your company as a class act or the event will backfire, with many candidates leaving with a sour taste in their mouths and telling everyone the next day that it was a bust.

Get as many of your high level management team involved in this event as possible. Have an introductory session that includes managers from different parts of the organization. Be sure to give attendees a chance to talk informally with people in the company who have backgrounds similar to their own. Whether you decide to conduct formal interviews during the open house is a matter of choice but often candidates attending an open house are there for an informal introduction to your company and did not come prepared to interview. Use your open house as an opportunity to publicize your company quickly through word of mouth.

There are several options for soliciting attendees. Some are by invitation only. Some are extremely large or conducted in small groups that arrive in specific time slots. However you decide to run your open house, the most important thing is that everyone leaves feeling good about your organization and the people they met.

Outplacement Services: Finally, let's look at one more overlooked source of hiring that is free and available to anyone. *Outplacement services* work with companies in the midst of layoffs to provide career counseling to the displaced workers. They are a great, free source of candidates. Some of the larger of these services include Right Associates, Manchester, and Drake Beam Morin, but there are many more.

Each of these services generally provides to the candidates a database of companies, such as yours, with open positions. If you have the internal resources to contact these companies directly, they will generally direct you to their website where you can post any number of positions, or allow you an opportunity to scan a database of available candidates currently exploring new opportunities. The outplacement services are not in the business of actually finding jobs for their clients so you must be proactive in using the databases they provide. They are paid by the companies doing the layoffs and not by the candidates, so they do not actively market the resumes of those they are counseling. However, with a little diligence, you can get a great return on very little investment.

Chapter 7, Agencies and Retained Search Firms

It is important first of all to define the differences between these two services. Agencies are organizations that help companies find employees and are paid *on a contingent basis*, meaning the company pays them if and when an employee is hired. Retained search firms, on the other hand, retain a fee up front to conduct a search to find a particular candidate. The term headhunter can apply to either type. To many who have spent much time on either side of the hiring fence, headhunters are at best a necessary evil, but to conduct an Intelligent Search, you must learn how and when to use these types of services.

I learned my trade in the agency world, and at another point in my career made my living in the retained search world. I owe what I know about my trade to both of those experiences and am still extremely grateful that in both instances I had a truly inspiring group of people from whom to learn. My co-workers were among the extraordinary ten percent of the recruiters in the world who cared enormously about the integrity of their profession and willingly walked from large fees when it infringed on their ethics. I still have many friends in both businesses.

This is a difficult chapter for me to write. Having been in each of those businesses, and then having spent eight years as an internal company recruiter, it is obvious to me that many companies overuse, misuse, and generally abuse both of these services and lose *hundreds of thousands of dollars* in the process. In addition to the monetary damage that is done, it is clear that most companies who call on these agents are woefully uninformed about the service they are actually buying.

I cringe at the stories I hear from most managers who buy lock, stock, and barrel, the stories told to them by the sellers of these services. Smart people who would not buy a car without thoroughly researching the product, do not even question who is on the other end of the phone call they receive from any agency. They gladly accept what they hear, in most instances, never even having met the broker they are about to let become a spokesperson for their company. Equally disturbing is the lack of understanding any of them have as to how the headhunting business works. Worst of all may be some of the tactics and practices that these agencies will use to get the business and the fees.

I am deliberately separating contingent agencies from retained search firms. While the fee structures do not differ dramatically, both asking a standard 25%-35% of the candidate's base salary, there is a significant difference in the service provided, the amount of leeway that's likely in the fee, and the terms of the contract. *Do not be misled by anyone in the contingent world who claims that they do both.* A firm that offers contingent services *should not be used* for retained search and you won't find a company that provides retained search that will work on a contingent basis. Let's first look at the world of agencies.

In the agency world there is a broad spectrum of what you can expect. The first rule of thumb is that the agency call *should not be your first call when you are filling any position.* Given all the alternatives that are more effective, using agencies as your first approach to filling a position is throwing money out the corporate window.

Second, be sure to *meet the agent who will be working with you.* This agent—if they're good—talks to hundreds of people a year. When they are working for you, they are hopefully talking about your company and able to describe it culturally, and in a positive way. Much damage can be done when you allow your company to be described by someone who has not taken the time to get to know anything about your organization. Here is a not so uncommon story as told to me by one company representative.

> *"I was working with this particular agency for the first time. On the phone, he gave me the usual pitch that he had five of what I was looking for and had just spoken to one of those candidates yesterday. While he claimed that the salary range I was working in was a little low, he knew the perfect guy for my position. Well, it somehow took three weeks for the agency to get me that perfect candidate's resume, leading me to believe he first started looking for someone like that right after he spoke to me. Worse yet, when I met the candidate, his resume did not reflect his true experience, he had left off a few jobs, and added some experience that was not a part of his background. When I asked him about the discrepancies, he very nonchalantly said I must be reading the resume from the agency as his resume didn't have that on it. I then asked him how the agency had contacted him—assuming he had been cold-called because of his experience—and he said that they had pulled his resume off the Internet. He never met anyone from that agency in person and when he had asked specifics about my company, he was directed to our website."*

Clearly this is not the kind of organization with whom your company should be working. While meeting the agent in person does not necessarily mean that you won't have a similar experience, you should be able to get a sense over lunch whether or not this is someone in whom you have *some* level of trust. Whatever your perception of her, it is most likely the same perception of potential candidates. If she claims to have a strong relationship with your company and makes a poor impression, it reflects negatively on you. Any quality candidate would rightly question why your company would be using someone of such poor integrity to find candidates.

The third rule of thumb is to be sure to negotiate the fee agreement in writing *before you've met any candidates.* An un-negotiated contract will hold you hostage if you meet a candidate that you like and decide you want to extend an offer. The fee agreement should be one that *you* have drawn up and not the fee agreement sent by the agency. *Fee agreements are negotiable 98% of the time*! Even in the market high times, you rarely need to pay the quoted 30% fee. Generally speaking, agencies will agree to 25% across the board. A few smaller ones will agree to 20% especially if you can guarantee payment within 30 days. There is also the possibility of paying whatever percentage is requested but negotiating a *"not to exceed"* clause. Other points that most agencies are willing to negotiate include longer or shorter pay periods and guarantee periods, length of time the referral stands as their referral, method of guarantee, and any other aspect you request, including an agreement to meet the candidate beforehand. This is not to say that agencies will roll over and take anything, but you should be able to negotiate important points that will benefit your recruiting goals. If the agency will not negotiate, *walk away*. There are hundreds of agencies and services out there and if they will not negotiate on the contract, they will be equally inflexible on any other points of contention.

A fourth recommendation when working with agencies is *always extend your own offer*. This suggestion assumes that whomever has responsibility to make the offer knows how to negotiate and will not "give away the farm" because the candidate asked for it, or for that matter, lose a good candidate because they couldn't bend or be creative. The major reason for extending your own offer is *not* because the agency fee is tied to the starting salary... although that is important. It is because this is the *most sensitive and revealing part of the entire hiring process.* How the candidate handles the negotiation phase will tell you an enormous amount about her and what you can expect in her performance, especially under pressure. I've met dozens of candidates that I thought the world of during the interview process and then lost interest in over the course of negotiating. Let the agency know that you will be extending an offer but do not lose the opportunity to learn what you can about this candidate by turning this step over to the agency. You can always call them into the process as a middleman after the offer has been extended to refine any points that need attention. To summarize, here are our four rules again:

1. The agency should not be your first option for filling positions.
2. Meet the agent who will be working with you.
3. Negotiate the fee agreement in writing before you meet any candidates.
4. Extend the offer yourself.

Another suggestion that must be emphasized when working with an agency is to consider *how the candidate is treated.* If the recruiter is willing to lose an offer to a candidate who really wants it, because of some picayune point of contention with you or your company, you should probably find another agency. Ask the candidate their impressions of the agency after you've brought them on board and take their comments seriously.

The agency world is a complicated one. Like any brokerage business, there is a huge world going on behind the scenes, one which you might not ever imagine. For example, even when you take the time to meet with the agency and show them around your facility—which I strongly recommend especially when your facility is impressive—you still may be working indirectly with someone you don't know and who doesn't know you. Many agencies, like realtors, do a fair amount of "split" business. They've gotten your position requirements or "job order," but they don't have a candidate. They call their personal network of recruiters and see if any of them are representing someone who fits the bill. Since they don't want to risk losing the job order by having the alternative agency contact you directly, they are cagey in all their descriptions to the candidate. Somehow they still work out the details, and a candidate shows up at your door who is not even being represented by the agency with whom you think you've built a relationship.

One of the most common misunderstandings I hear from managers is "You should call this agency. He has a lot of these candidates." What lay people who have not made a living within the agency world fail to understand is that *the agencies have to say they have candidates in order to get your job order*. Along the same lines, they usually tell candidates they have jobs exactly like whatever they describe or at salaries much higher than what they currently earn. In order to be successful, they need to "collect" as many job orders and candidates as they can, and hope for some matches along the way, again, much like realtors. Any internal recruiter or HR department will tell you that it is normal to field as many as 10-20 agency calls every month, and much more than that if you run an ad that draws attention to your company needs. It is also not at all surprising to take half an hour or more to negotiate all of the fine points of the agreement and describe your needs, and never see a single resume or hear from the agency again.

Another troubling aspect of the agency world that is being opened by the Internet world is the number of resumes you can see from an agency when they have never even spoken to the candidate. They can pull the resume, send it to you, and then if you have an interest, call the candidate to get more information and hear if they might be interested in your position. It will be interesting in coming years to see how this aspect of the agency business will develop. One way to avoid this pitfall is to make effective use of the Internet yourself and to avoid opening a position to any agency until you have researched available candidates on your Internet sites.

With all this said, when should you use an agency, if ever? Much depends on the structure of the rest of your recruiting efforts. If you are successfully using the Internet and your employee referral program, or if you have an internal recruiting team, agencies should be your last call and a rarity at that. Under any circumstances, you should allow two to four weeks of Internet search just to cull any resumes from those sources. This will prevent your paying a $20,000 fee for someone you could have pulled off an Internet site or who is the best friend of one of your own co-workers.

If you've built a successful internal recruiting team, as the next chapter describes, you should almost never be using agencies. If you feel you've exhausted your own more cost-effective resources including searching your own database of resumes and candidates interviewed in the past, it may be time to use a few agencies. The guidelines you outline for these agencies should be understood and followed by whichever agencies you choose. Picking agencies is like finding candidates. Your best bets are those that have been spoken highly of by your own employees. There will never be a shortage of these services so there is no reason to feel that you need to use anyone with whom you are not comfortable working on a long-term basis. Narrow your choices to three firms. If you've had no results within three weeks, the most obvious reason is that your qualifications for the position are unrealistic. An agency can help you by sharing with you how often they have seen candidates with those qualifications in the past. If the answer is never, you're barking up the wrong tree, and must re-define your position qualifications.

I would hesitate to ever use an agency when there will also be relocation fees involved in hiring the right candidate and I would make that clear to the agency up front. Otherwise your out of pocket costs for a candidate who may need to either return home after six months, or leave your company for whatever reason, are astronomical. On the other hand, if you are working with an agency that has a national network like most of the bigger ones do, they may find someone from another area for you who is already re-locating to your area at their own expense due to a spousal relocation.

One of the times that an agency can be successful for you is when you are hiring into or out of a part of the country where your own company network does not reach. National agencies tend to know which areas of the country are hotbeds for different skills and can better target those areas. For example, while medical systems development might be a rare skill in your locale it could be plentiful in another part of the country.

There is a final point to consider on behalf of the agencies. As explained at the beginning of this chapter, agencies are overused, misused, and *abused*. I've heard— and lived—my share of hellish stories about what agencies do to companies. However I've heard an equal number of horror stories of what companies do to agencies. Anyone who has worked in an agency for any amount of time knows of a few times that they were the ones burned.

For example, a company contracts their services, is shown a few quality candidates, and extends no offers. Three months later the agency learns that the company waited a few weeks, called the candidates directly, brought them back in, and hired them without paying a fee. Very often, because agencies and headhunters tend to carry reputations that are not always admirable, companies feel they have a right to take advantage of them. *Once you've contracted the agency services and definitely once you've interviewed a candidate through them, you are obligated to pay the agreed upon fee.* Never mind that one of the candidates is the brother of your CEO. Shame on you for not having explored those avenues before calling the agencies.

When I was in the agency world, I once worked with a company that extended the candidate an offer and told the candidate not to tell me or they wouldn't get the offer. I know of another company who would collect resumes from me and then pass them to a friend in another agency and then interview the person through the other agency. I know companies who don't want to pay the fee after they've met the candidate because "After all, you didn't do anything except send me a resume, why should I pay $12,000 for that?"

This shallow attitude neglects to consider the years it takes for a recruiter to build a strong base of business and the number of people spoken with on an annual basis who never collect any fees for the agent. While the agencies do not have a magic bullet for getting candidates that you can't get yourself, better recruiters will continually cultivate relationships with candidates for years that may not culminate in a placement for the first few years of their discussions. Again, like the realtor, the actual service provided by a recruiter sometimes seems out of proportion to the fees that are being requested. What the company does not see is the years and years of building relationships that a recruiter works to be successful in his profession. And beware that cheating an agency out of a fee that they've legitimately earned can do your company more damage than whatever the savings were worth. Recruiters talk to hundreds of candidates every year and can give your company a bad reputation that might cost you important potential hires.

There are numerous cases each year of companies who work only with agencies that provide some sort of kickback or special treats. While this practice is illegal, most recruiters know which companies are guilty of this habit and could blow the whistle at any time on those company representatives. Many managers may not consider it a "kickback" to be taken to a private golf course by a particular agency, but in actuality, it is. If a manager in your organization insists on using an outside service rather than your own internal resources to hire, it may be worth a discussion to understand why.

There is also a steady practice of using agencies to "launder" the raiding of a competitive company. While it may be too sticky to try to recruit a high ranking executive who works at a company where one of your board members works, having an agency call that candidate can leave you with clean hands. All in all, there is a significant amount of dirt thrown on both sides of the tracks in the agency world, and you should be aware of what you are getting into when you contact contingent agencies.

Retained Search Firms: With *retained search* firms, you'll find a horse of an entirely different color. Many of the issues surrounding the agency world are not a part of the retained search world due to the nature of the payment. When you call a retained search firm to help fill a position, you can expect to pay one third of the payment up front, another third halfway through the search, and the final third on successful completion of the search. It is not at all unusual for these payouts which generally run 30%-35% of the candidate's salary or sometimes, entire compensation package, to run into six figures for very senior level positions.

A retained search firm works more like a talent scout than an agency. Just as fees for finding and recruiting great sports figures or actors is high, so are the fees for retained search. Once the search has begun and the paperwork is signed, you are committed to payment regardless of whether you find the candidate through your own devices or theirs. So what is the search firm doing to earn those fees? *Nothing that you couldn't teach someone in your internal recruiting department to do for you if your company decided to save that money.*

I really enjoyed the retained search world. It was organized and methodical. Gathering the requirements from all parties involved in the final hiring decision was critical. Pointing out discrepancies in what one person thought was important versus another was an important part of the pre-search. Making sure all parties were in agreement as to those requirements was essential. Paying attention to hidden hostilities or agendas among those parties could mean the difference between success and failure. Ironing those points out before beginning the search was a crucial pre-requisite.

Every search starts the same way. The requirements are clearly defined; the company culture is understood; fee agreements are signed; the candidate compensation package is outlined, and then the search begins. First, the retained firm will identify all the companies that are in competitive businesses and likely to have a candidate on board with those qualifications. The search may be defined as local, national, or global. Round two includes using their own network of industry professionals and other research resources to begin making calls and getting the word out regarding the position. Over the course of these calls, they begin to gather names of contenders. The company receives reports on a weekly or bi-weekly basis regarding the summation of these calls and potential candidates.

The potential candidates are called, narrowing the field to three or four top choices who are interested and qualified. Interviews are scheduled for those chosen and on completion, an offer is extended. If the offer is accepted, the search is completed. If not, back to round one and the search continues. Anywhere along the way, the search firm will provide intelligence information that they can pick up including reputation of the hiring company, reasons that qualified candidates may or may not be interested, and the attractiveness of the position and the compensation package.

There are many times that a company can and should take advantage of a retained search firm. However, retained search is a hefty financial proposition and one that is not within reach of every company budget. For those organizations that can afford these fees, using a retained search firm is a good idea at the most senior levels within the organization. Bear in mind that the representative you are meeting probably has nothing to do with actually conducting the search and is really the go-between in maintaining the client relationship, and supervising the search process.

There are hundreds of retained search firms around the country. The more well-known the reputation, the more costly the search. There are also dozens of retained search firms with less recognizable names that are within your own local area. Whichever you choose, be sure to get references, and ideally those where similar positions within comparable companies were filled. When calling these references ask how long the search took. Are they still satisfied with the candidate hired? Would they use the same retained firm again in the future?

For companies that cannot afford these services, the skills it takes to conduct a retained search can be learned by any intelligent recruiter interested in listening, learning, and following the process. While there are several training programs that teach a recruiter how to be a recruiter, none are widely available that provide training on conducting retained searches. It is a trade that is perpetuated and refined solely within the retained search firms. But if you have an internal recruiting team, you may want to consider the option of dedicating a recruiter to these more senior level searches.

Chapter 8, Building an Effective Internal Recruiting Team

Throughout the preceding chapters, I've referred several times to an internal recruiting team. While the term is fairly self-explanatory, there are many questions as to how, when, and why a company might want to consider this option. It also begs the question of what makes a recruiting team different than a human resources group? It is important to differentiate the responsibilities of an internal recruiting team versus the more standard human resource department.

Your internal recruiting team is a team focused solely on finding, evaluating, and hiring new talent into the company. Once the person is on board, the responsibility for these employees becomes the focus of your HR department. The purpose of an internal recruiting team is to bring in-house all the efforts that would otherwise be directed to outside hiring services. An internal recruiting team ensures that you are taking your own company needs into consideration and making every attempt to satisfy them. As an internal resource they are not being shared by multiple companies, not being directed by outside influences, and have no conflict of interest in allegiance or motivation.

While this idea may seem relatively new to many organizations, in the technical world it is a fairly common practice to have internal recruiters separate from your HR department. How should you decide when it is time to build this function internally? There are several indicators:

- Are you spending over $100,000/year on agency fees?
- Do you consistently make over 60 hires per year?

- Is your hiring process totally decentralized among many people?
- Is there a centralized resume database? Does it get used on a regular basis to conduct searches or is it just a resume repository?
- Is there a single person or team who holds primary responsibility for reaching the company hiring goals?

In answering these questions, it becomes clear whether or not it is time to consider hiring your first internal recruiter. If you answer yes to the first three questions and no to the final two, it is time to seriously consider bringing this function in-house. Finding the right person for this job becomes the next challenge and one that could require a number of interviews.

Where do you start looking for your first recruiter? The first recruiter you hire will be the most critical member of your team. Just as you would not hire your first sales person without sales experience, you cannot expect to build a successful recruiting effort with junior recruiters or someone who is transitioning into recruiting. There is too much for them to learn and no one in your organization capable of mentoring them. The ideal candidate for your first recruiter will meet the following criteria:

- Seven or more years experience with that time spent exclusively in a recruiting role, *not human resources*. This is not meant to denigrate the HR profession but the skills involved in the two areas are dramatically different, and this is born out by the fact that few folks seem to excel at both.
- At least a portion of their experience should come from having been successful in the agency world.

- They should have received formal recruiter training very early on in their recruiting career.
- They should be excited about being a recruiting professional and view themselves as sales people.
- They must have exceptional communication skills both verbal and written.
- They must be someone you will be proud to have act as an ambassador for your organization.
- They must be outgoing, or at least able to project an outgoing nature when required.

The most likely source for the first hire is to find someone who has already successfully built an internal recruiting team for another company. The second most likely avenue is to consider someone in the agency world— possibly even someone that has been successful as an outside vendor to your organization. If you have a particular agency with whom you've struck up a successful relationship, you should probably entertain the possibility of having one of their agents join you.

What can you expect to pay? Once you've identified potential candidates, you must structure a compensation package that will provide a base salary but also provide incentive based on specific hiring metrics. The structure of the compensation package will vary based on different parts of the country and how much experience the candidate brings with them. Do not expect to pay them as you would your HR staff members. It is more likely their compensation package should resemble that of your sales team to some degree.

It is not unusual to see base salaries for experienced recruiters in the $50K-$75K range. Additional incentives should bring the overall package near the six-figure mark or better. If your first reaction to these numbers is a sense of shock, then you must revisit your current hiring costs. Beyond these numbers, take a hard look at how long it takes to fill each position and what the loss of that hire can cost your organization. Take another look at retention of those hires and figure out what that turnover costs your company. Next calculate how many agency fees were paid for people who left your organization within a year. To be really accurate, figure out how many people hired with agency fees, left because the same agency placed them somewhere else. With all of these costs properly evaluated, if you go back to the compensation package for your internal recruiter, you will see it is much more justifiable. Many companies that expect to pay a recruiter as they pay HR do not understand the difference in skills sets; too often these are the same organizations that have no objection to paying agencies large fees for the same skills. Putting the skill set and compensation in its proper perspective will eventually lead the way to an Intelligent Search strategy.

Now that you've hired your first recruiter, to whom should they report? The reporting structure for your recruiter is a difficult decision. If they report directly to any manager, they tend to have a conflict of interest in their attempts to fairly fill positions across the organization with no partiality to their own manager's needs. If they report to HR, you'll have what restaurants experience as the "night shift/day shift" dilemma. While the two functions *seem* an obvious team, in reality they have goals that often cloud the picture when it comes to successful recruiting. To complicate the issue, the compensations are often vastly different and this creates internal hostility. If a senior level executive such as the CEO in the organization is also heavily involved in the ability of the company to attract good people—as all senior executives should be—then they may be the logical reporting point. There are some organizations where recruiting works so closely with sales that the VP of sales may be the best place for your recruiter to report. Another option is to have the recruiting department report to the same person to whom HR reports. With internal recruiting teams still in their infancy, this is a challenge that must be addressed by each organization individually.

What expectations should you have of a recruiter's performance? How should you measure their success? As the concept of internal recruiting teams has flourished, the metrics that a good recruiter is measured against have also become more sophisticated. Initially, the only way a company measured the performance of a recruiter was by volume. The assumption was that the more hires, the better the recruiter.

As the field matured, it became obvious that there were many more significant factors to consider. Let's say Recruiter A hires 60 people in one year, and Recruiter B hires 40. The initial conclusion is that Recruiter A is the better recruiter. But as you look more carefully, another story may emerge. Suppose you dig further and find out that Recruiter A hired 20 of those hires through agencies, and Recruiter B only hired two through agencies. Then consider that the hires by Recruiter A showed a significantly shorter stay with the organization than those hired by Recruiter B. Now the numbers have shifted. Furthermore, imagine that one of your metrics is a quality metric and the hires made by Recruiter B consistently demonstrate more upward mobility and success in your company than Recruiter A. At this point, which recruiter rates higher?

For some companies, the answer may still be Recruiter A. There are companies where all those other factors simply do not matter and the only measure of success is number of hires. That is a totally acceptable decision as long as you are aware that *there are recruiting metrics that may matter more than just the number of hires.*

The important lesson is an old one: *know thyself.* Once you know which metrics are most important to your organization, structuring the incentive portion of the compensation will be much clearer because you need to encourage the behaviors that matter the most to your organization. There are literally hundreds of different compensation packages for recruiters and the business of internal recruiting is still new enough that you will probably need to be creative in designing one that works best for you and your recruiters.

At this stage, what should you expect of your Recruiter? Your recruiter should easily take on the management of all of your recruitment efforts including position descriptions, advertising needs, recruiting budget, centralizing your recruiting efforts under one person, and satisfying as many of your hiring needs as possible without sacrificing company values or quality. That person will need to centralize your recruiting files—not to be confused or mixed with your HR files—and be able to identify which candidates should be contacted on a regular basis and which should be classified as closed doors.

Your recruiter should streamline the interviewing process, be involved in coaching managers on interviewing tips and techniques when appropriate, and be very involved in the operations of the organization. *This requires that upper management include the recruiter in any functions that will discuss future hiring needs and issues that will impact the efforts of the recruiter to successfully fill company positions.* Your recruiter will only be as successful as you let them be by keeping them involved in the business of the organization. It is essential to their success that the management team support their efforts.

Over the next few years the recruiter should gradually phase out use of agencies by expanding the employee referral program and increasing Internet hiring. Within the first two to three years, you should see a significant reduction in money spent on agency fees. In the meantime, because your recruiter should be able to determine when a candidate may fit multiple opportunities within the company, they can focus on minimizing the number of interviews and return visits required to extend an offer. This will decrease the interview cycle and increase your hiring as your offers will be extended on a more timely basis to quality candidates. Your recruiter must slowly re-define— with the cooperation of everyone involved—who will be involved in interviews and draw the line on excessive interviewing. The recruiter must work closely with the management team to encourage cooperation with quicker turnaround hiring as one of the mutual objectives. If your management team struggles with feedback provided by the recruiter, remember that the candidate is sharing his perceptions with the recruiter and the recruiter's only interest should be in improving your overall hiring process.

What does your recruiter do first? Many companies are under the misimpression that the way an internal recruiter is most effective is by searching for what the industry calls the "passive looker." This subject is analyzed more thoroughly in the next chapter, but suffice to say, that while one of the objectives of your internal recruiter is to develop relationships with candidates for future hiring as well as present needs, the more immediate demands of satisfying current openings is not through those relationships, but through the sources we've already discussed in this book.

At this point there should be less confusion over what your internal recruiter is doing to earn their position and compensation. Now you may be saying "What will the HR department do now?" The answer most likely is, a better job. Your HR department, now freed of hiring responsibility, can focus their attentions on issues involving benefits analysis, employee relations, company image and corporate activities, legal issues, and naturalization considerations. Many of these more detailed responsibilities will make your company more attractive and keep you out of hot water as you continue to grow.

When do you decide it is time to add to your recruiting team? Your recruiter will have a good sense of when he or she is overwhelmed but one sure indicator is when you are hiring more than 60 full time permanent professionals a year. Depending on what your first recruiter needed to do to get the recruiting function up to speed and showing a marked improvement, even over 40 hires may indicate the need for a second recruiter. Another metric to determine when to add to the recruiting team is to ask the following series of questions surrounding timing issues:

- How many days does it take to acquire the resumes from the various job sites, after the time of initial posting?
- How many days does it take between acquiring the resume and making the first call to the potential candidate?
- How long before the candidates are scheduled for interviews?
- How long from the first interview to the offer/decline stage?
- How long is the entire recruiting lifecycle from posting the request to making an offer?

While there are no right or wrong answers to these questions, the reality is that *timing is the name of the game in recruiting quality candidates*. As a professional recruiter, I consider it unacceptable if the resume isn't pulled and the call isn't made within 48 hours of initial posting. Taking more than five days to schedule an interview is too long. More than ten days to complete the entire process shows room for improvement. This is not to say your recruiter is not doing a great job but these are signs of recruiter overload that may indicate the need for more help.

At this point the decision also becomes whether the added resource would be more beneficial as an Internet researcher working with the recruiter or as a second recruiter. Bringing an Internet researcher on board, frees up the two or three hours a day that the recruiter may be spending on the Internet and allows them that time for more interviewing.

One way that many companies supplement their recruiting needs during an aggressive hiring thrust is to bring on a temporary contract recruiter. This practice has its pros and cons. While it appears on the surface to solve temporary hiring demands, the full impact should be understood. The temporary recruiter will be long gone— sometimes with your database or internal company directory—long before you have time to assess their performance beyond the most basic issue of volume. At times when this is an absolute necessity, a strong suggestion would be to try to bring back someone who may have been with the company in the past, maybe even a retiree. In the long run they will be better able to discuss your organization, have a loyalty to your goals and long-term objectives, and be accountable to a degree, for future success.

It should be obvious by now that I am a strong proponent of building an internal recruiting function. The loyalty of a good recruiting team will enhance the image of any company and improve hiring statistics. While it has become standard for companies to say, "attracting and retaining quality employees is key to our organization," these are empty words if they're not backed up by actions and the best action you can take is to build a highly skilled internal recruiting team.

Chapter 9, Recruiting the "Passive Looker"

In the latter 1990s, recruiting departments were all under the microscope especially in the technical world where the huge demands for talent, forced us all to focus on how to recruit better. The market was tight, candidates were in high demand, and every company was squeezing the recruiting pipeline to meet our incredible hiring needs. As we move through 2001, recruiting is once again under the microscope but for totally different reasons. The tidal wave of demand for technical expertise in many companies has diminished to a trickle and we are all particularly cost conscious on where recruiting dollars are being spent. On the other hand, in the healthcare world, the heat is building and many hospitals and healthcare facilities are using practices new to them to hire nurses, that were common in the technical hiring world. Any discrepancy in supply and demand hiring forces new ways of doing business.

Whichever side of the coin is currently face-up, there has been much written and discussed within the trade about recruiting the "passive looker." This is a person who is not looking for a job, not attending job fairs, not posting their resume on job boards, not calling a local headhunter, and not responding to companies advertising. They are sitting at their desk, more or less comfortable with their current employer, and not actively involved in any job search… but they are willing to talk if you call.

The conventional wisdom is that by cold calling those candidates, a recruiter can increase their pipeline and have a high quality prospect ready for any position. There is a good deal of push from management teams in all companies to encourage their internal recruiting teams to go after these candidates, as they've read many articles espousing this type of recruiting.

Historically, the passive looker was a term invented by the world of professional headhunters. The professional headhunter would call industry hotshots on a regular basis to understand what might motivate them to jump ship, and thus keep a fertile "farm" of candidates to call when an opportunity arose that may match their qualifications. For a professional headhunter, these candidates were also potential clients at any time so there was considerable incentive to make calls to passive lookers on a regular basis. It also became a handy marketing tool to encourage a client to use the headhunter services as they were reaching "passive lookers" that all the advertising dollars in the world would not reach.

So how does this effort help the average company recruiter looking for specific skill sets that can be "activated" with quick turnaround whenever needed? To answer that question, it must be broken into two categories. The first are the senior level positions with compensation packages over $100,000 and the second are the more common positions below that level.

Positions that are high-level management or critical senior roles within an organization, lend themselves very well to this type of search. At senior levels this is likely the most common way that a CEO, CIO, VP, or director makes a career move. That call may be generated from their own personal network, a retained search firm, a headhunter in the contingent world, or a direct company recruiter acting as a company representative. His or her name and position are clearly listed in the annual report, on an Internet site, or in some other public forum, possibly a quote in a news article or a presentation at an industry conference. Nevertheless, the busy executive has done nothing on his part to begin a job search. A specific call, however, has teased him into considering another possibility and when that possibility expands into a genuine interest in the position described, he is now fully engaged in the steps toward a new employer. He is no longer a passive looker.

Let's look more closely at the second scenario where the passive looker may be a web designer with specific programming language experience. He works at Company A, which consists of 200 employees, 120 of them are technical professionals, and 60 of them are web designers. Now the recruiter's job becomes more complicated. Before he even begins to call them, he must first get their names from a company confidential listing, or by running through voice-mail extensions owned by one company until he hits the right group of extensions, or he may have networked over the years and know one name to get him started. Often they will call the receptionist at the front desk and through misrepresentation, get that person to release a few names as a starting point. Another possibility is that someone at the company has recently been interviewed in a local industry paper and those few names start the calls. Once the recruiter is "in the castle" he can proceed, through simple charisma or outright scheming to get one phone number after another until he's contacted almost all 60 web designers.

Now look at the numbers. Of those 60 web designers, six may express an interest, three of them are curious and tire kicking, and the other three are truly interested. However, since they did nothing to generate a job search, chances are these candidates are difficult to schedule, often cancel their interviews, and most importantly, expect a significant salary increase because after all they say, "You called me."

How much time has that recruiter spent so far to reach these three potential candidates? Do you have that amount of time to fill your positions? How many calls do you estimate it took to get through the process? How do you think that call sounds from the candidate perspective when the recruiter made 100 of them in a few days? Is that call enthusiastic and giving a positive impression of your company? Or does that call sound more like the incessant telemarketing solicitation calls that we each receive at home every day? How many of those calls are so compelling that the name of the caller and vendor sticks in your mind when you are ready to buy? These are all elements to weigh when the suggestion to recruit the passive looker is considered.

Is there a time and place for making passive looker calls to the group of candidates who are not at the most senior level? Definitely. They are great calls to make during "down" times to introduce your company. They make sense when a recruiter can fit in a half a dozen calls a week around their other more active candidate sources. They are a real benefit when the call reaps a relationship that may be of value down the road. However, the rewards of passive looker or true cold calls are very minimal on a quick turnaround basis and make more sense as a gradual, long-term component of your contact strategy.

Lastly, there is one important point to keep in mind. If you've ever been the company on the receiving end of a recruiter who is canvassing through your phone directory to recruit someone away, it is, to put it kindly, infuriating. When you live in a tightly connected community, as most markets are, it is unpleasant and borders on socially irresponsible. Do you want your recruiters drawing talent from local companies with whom you hope to someday do business? How receptive do you think they'll be to your business partnership when you've just raided their technical talent? While we all need to find the top talent, "Do Unto Others…" is still a motto that serves us well throughout our business interactions.

Chapter 10, The Interview and Offer Process

Once upon a time there was a candidate with ten years of experience in the technical world who had worked in some very sophisticated technological environments and who was well known in the industry as a top-notch talent. In the course of his career changes, he told me the following story.

> *"I interviewed at a huge pharmaceutical firm on the East Coast. My resume had been brought to the attention of one of the hiring managers towards the end of February as an employee referral of a friend. My first interview was in April. Because the company was very well known and highly touted as a great place to work, I was excited. I met with three representatives, all of whom told me in the interview process, that they needed all of the skills I had and I had come highly recommended by more than one person within the organization. I waited for the next step and received a call in May to schedule a second round of interviews. The earliest I could be squeezed into the schedule of the appropriate parties was early June. I interviewed again in early June and again was told by the HR representative and one of the interviewers that they were very interested in me.*
>
> *I waited. And waited. After a few weeks, I called HR and was told they needed me to come back and meet two or three more people, bringing the count to about eight. This time the schedule was arranged within a week and I finished that*

interview the first week in July. Again I waited with no word and not wanting to appear to be bugging HR, called my friend and asked him to find out what the holdup was. He was told by everyone that they really wanted to hire me. By now, he was feeling a little foolish but told me to hang in as sometimes it takes longer for big companies to make decisions.

By mid-July I still hadn't heard and was slowly losing enthusiasm as I could only imagine that if it took this long to hire one person, how long it would take to make other decisions within the organization. By now I wouldn't even have thought to contact HR but I received a call one day saying, yes they wanted to extend an offer but the people who needed to sign off on that were on summer vacation. Could I wait a week or two? I agreed. At this point I had received a promotion at my current job and was re-considering whether I should leave.

Now it was mid-August and I finally received a call saying they were ready to go forward but due to organizational changes I would need to come back and meet one final manager. I debated telling them I was no longer interested, but as I had already invested seven months in this process, decided to see it through. Once again there were vacation delays. The interview finally took place at the very end of August and they were ready to make an offer.

One week later I still had no verbal offer let alone a written one. The following week I received a call from HR who extended what I considered to be a generous verbal offer. While at this stage, I was not as interested in leaving my current company as I had been, I still considered the offer. I was told that the offer was contingent on my passing a drug test and a physical that needed to be scheduled by a different group. The first available appointment was the third week in September. I scheduled it, showed up, and did what I needed to do. I was told the results could take a few weeks.

Meantime, in my current company I was due for my annual performance review where I received a surprisingly significant increase, narrowing the gap between my new offer and my current salary to a very small margin. In the second week in October, I was told that all my tests were fine and the company was ready to establish a start date. At this point, I was having major concerns as to whether my career was ready for a company that would take so long to come to one hiring conclusion, so I called up my friend and told him my reservations. He informed me that his group had been merged with another pharmaceutical firm, and while he still thinks it's a great place to work, he is concerned about the merger and how it would affect his own job security.

I guess that was the final straw. I called the representative and expressed my extreme apologies that I would be declining the offer. She was very understanding and said that she understood that their interview process was long and drawn out and a lot of things can happen over the course of it. My friend subsequently informed me that a few of the managers were a little peeved that I pulled out at the last minute. While I hoped I had made the right decision, in looking back over the process, I was amazed that I had put up with the time span it took to come to the offer stage."

Amazingly, this is not an unusual tale for a recruiter to hear. And notice that this is just the phase *after recruiting* a prospect! One of the key successes to hiring quality candidates is the *timeliness of the interview to offer process*. In the course of interviewing and hiring, companies share this common challenge. Companies that provide guidelines such as "no more than two weeks from interview process to offer" are more likely to succeed. Yet another improvement is to have a guideline on *how long it should take between receipt of a resume and first interview.*

To overcome these challenges, everyone in the interview process must know their exact role and timing expectations. While this challenge is more easily overcome in smaller companies through management training, the larger the company is, the more difficult this task becomes. In most large corporations, the inability to hire as quickly as would be desired, is due in part to the nightmare of the scheduling. Making it even more difficult is that the team of interviewers changes on a regular basis. Almost all managers believe they are good interviewers. But in my experience, less than half are even slightly cognizant of what must transpire over the course of the interview process. Very few give candidate interviewing the priority on their schedules that it deserves.

Starting from that very general point, *the interview schedules* that are responsible for coordinating all of your company interviews are probably a supreme challenge. Those involved in the interview process let themselves be delayed, rarely read the resume on more than a cursory level, and are relatively unprepared for the interview itself. Curiously—or is it?—the managers who are most vocal in their inability to fill their positions are those most guilty of having no availability on their schedules to conduct a fair interview.

One of the most valuable modifications any company can make to meet their hiring objectives, is to agree that there are two or three days and times that anyone involved in the interview process agrees to be available for any interviews. This time should be blocked out as preciously as any meeting or conference call and adhered to as seriously as any other events on the agenda. Not only does this make the schedulers task easier as they know towards which days to steer candidate interviews, but the commitment of time from the interviewers assures that no candidate is left waiting in a lobby for 45 minutes as their first impression of your company. Equally important is that everyone involved in the interview process adhere to their allotted time, keeping the others in the process on their schedules. The manager who needs more than an hour of time for an interview, generally needs more training on what should be accomplished in the interview process.

I've never heard of any company that hired professional candidates solely on the basis of one interview with one company representative. So what is the ideal number to have involved in the hiring process? In the world of sports, no one expects one player to be the quarterback, receiver, and defense. On your interviewing team there are various positions that must be played and no one interviewer is responsible for making all the hiring decisions. Your interview team may consist of your HR or recruiting rep, the reporting manager, a senior member or peer of the candidate, and a final specialty interview to further qualify the candidate skills. At more senior levels, it may make sense to bring a candidate back for a final interview especially when there are two or three finalists and one common person is conducting these comparative interviews.

When I hear a company tell me that they brought the same candidate back four and five times, each time with multiple interviewers—which is not at all uncommon in large corporations—I shudder. Many intelligent people would begin to question the company's ability to make a final judgment. *This challenge to the interview process can be corrected if upper management gets training in how to interview.* Once your interview process is pruned down to two visits and five interviewers, with only special exceptions, you'll see a dramatic difference in the turnaround on filling your positions.

Interviewing Tips

There are some great books on interviewing that go far beyond the intention of this book. But based on the hundreds of thousands of dollars it takes a company to find and schedule candidates, it is worth mentioning a few basic interviewing rules that every company should understand and follow. Here are some of the interview rules that are violated most often:

- Sell the candidate on the company. Understand that the interview is a two way street and both parties should be doing as much "selling" as learning. Too often managers assume they are conducting the interview and don't bother to get them excited about the position and the job responsibilities.
- Make the candidate comfortable. Each candidate who leaves your company interview is going to tell ten people about it. The impression each of you leaves may be the only impression of your company this candidate ever talks about for the rest of his career. Make it good.
- Gather information. Interviews must be used to gather information from the candidate. Of course, it matters if you like the candidate, but can he do the job, and just as important, is he interested in what you have to offer? Over and

---

over I've seen managers finish interviews with very little idea what the candidate has accomplished beyond the resume level.

- Review the resume. Take at least five minutes to review the resume before meeting the candidate. You don't need to critique it and analyze every word, but at least know the content and use it as a guideline, not as the gospel word of everything this candidate has experienced. I've seen great candidates write lousy resumes. Upon closer investigation, there may be experiences in the candidate's career that are not on the resume.

- Hold your calls and E-mails. Put your phone calls on hold during the interview and focus on the candidate. The same rule applies to E-mail. Many managers have the mistaken impression that it's acceptable to reply to incoming E-mails while they are conducting an interview. This can only be perceived by the candidate as a lack of respect for the hiring decision, a decision that may be of the utmost importance to them.

- Be honest. Let the candidate know your impressions. If you feel his experience is not strong enough in a certain area for your position, give him the opportunity for rebuttal. Maybe you focused on other parts of his experience and he hasn't had the chance to highlight that particular area.

Establish a company guideline as to how long it takes to extend an offer, once the interview process is complete. Dragging out a decision is unfair to the candidate and her other job opportunities. Decisions that cannot be made in a reasonable time are a good indication that the candidate is not a good fit. Saying no to a candidate that everyone liked is not going to destroy your company reputation. However, leaving them hanging on through the interview process month after month can do serious damage to your organization.

Extending an Offer

Extending the offer and negotiating the hiring terms are among the most critical components of the recruiting process. Negotiation skills are not learned overnight—just ask any salesperson. Successful negotiation takes years and years to refine. However, most companies have no training at all on how to successfully extend an offer and close the deal. This is the most delicate part of the entire hiring process and it is often left to novices. Here again, are some basic tips in negotiating offers:

- Who should extend? The person who spent the most time with the candidate is the most likely person to successfully negotiate an offer. In most cases this will be your HR rep or recruiter. In many companies, it is considered prestigious to have a senior partner or management member extend the offer. The problem with this approach is that they really don't know the candidate well enough to be handling this phase of the process. They have not been with him from the first call and have certainly not earned the confidence of that candidate or established rapport.

- Don't create surprises. The offer negotiation begins on a very subtle level in the first phone call with a candidate. While the final decision on what to offer may come down to the last interviews, the candidate should not be too surprised at that point as to what to expect. If her expectations were wildly out of line during the interview process, it needs to be addressed before the offer is formally extended. You can casually ask the candidate on what considerations their expectation is set. You can also ask in a very straightforward way, that if the company may not be able to meet those objectives, would she prefer to end the interview process now? By meeting these initial discussions head on, the final offer will not be a surprise.

- Know your candidate's career goals. Many times a candidate has no idea what your company compensation structure will support but they feel you will lowball them if they don't quote an expectation higher than even their wildest wishes, just as many sellers do with their homes. Whatever they say about salary expectations may not be anywhere near as important as meeting their short and long-term career goals.

- Appreciate the sensitivity of these negotiations. Do not expect a candidate to be able to effectively respond to your verbal offer if they are in an area that offers them no confidentiality or they are at home with a baby screaming in the background. Ask when is a good time to discuss a potential offer.

- Know their "magic" number. As best as possible, know what the magic number is that will definitely close the candidate. Even if you are unable or unwilling to meet this number, at least know the target.

- Be sure of your options. Sometimes a candidate has you over a barrel because his skills are so limited in the marketplace that you won't find another like him. Be sure to apprise yourself of market considerations during the negotiation.

- Be prepared to counter with other-than-salary alternatives. You may want to negotiate with any number of alternatives including more vacation, stock options, sign-on bonus, earlier or later start date, and at more senior levels, severance packages.

- Know your company guidelines. Nothing is worse to a candidate than telling him you can get something you cannot. For instance, benefits like a 401k plan are governed by federal regulations that you cannot influence.

- Keep the negotiation friendly. No matter how stressed you feel during the negotiation, keep it friendly. If you reach an impasse and can't compromise, let them know in the nicest way that you see no way to move forward in the negotiation but you'd hope both sides could keep an open mind should the situation change in the future.

The interview is an important, sensitive part of the process that requires attention from all members of your organization. Treat it accordingly. Make it a priority to set guidelines and provide training and your hiring will improve dramatically.

Chapter 11, Summary and Final Thoughts

You've read thus far that the concept of an Intelligent Search is as much about *the order* of your search as it is about *how* to conduct your search. Of course, not every company can use all the ideas we've suggested, but hopefully any company can incorporate at least one or two new ideas and significantly improve their hiring productivity. To summarize, your two best sources of hiring are a strong employee referral program and an aggressive approach to Internet recruiting. There are many companies who have turned their hiring statistics upside down by expanding these two areas. Here's a typical experience:

> *"In the early 1990s, over 40% of our hiring was through agencies. By building an internal recruiting team, substantially increasing our employee referral program, and continually improving our Internet hiring, we dropped agency hiring to under 2%. By the year 2000, over 40% of our hiring was employee referrals, and over 40% was Internet research."*

Outplacement services are a highly overlooked source of free hiring. Job fairs are a great addition to your recruiting formula if you find the right ones for you. An open house can add tremendously to the mix of your annual hiring especially during peak hiring times.

The interview process itself must be a clear-cut, streamlined process with a quick turnaround. Negotiating the offer is often the most neglected part of the entire hiring process and should be one that is given the most attention.

Finally, it is important to keep a sense of community in all of your hiring efforts. There is a big difference between raiding a neighboring company and creating a strong employee referral program that gives your company every competitive advantage that you have earned. Raiding other companies does not lend itself to strong community ties and in any business today, the world is too small to create enemies. Hiring while maintaining a sense of community is a delicate balancing act that you should re–evaluate periodically. Particularly with regard to staffing, the advantages of being a good neighbor in the business community will invariably pay off over time.

Pamela Ciccantelli

PART 2: CANDIDATE SEARCH

Pamela Ciccantelli

Chapter 12, Introduction

If you're on the flip side of the employment market, looking for a job or a whole new career, you too have much to gain from learning how to conduct an Intelligent Search. From your perspective an Intelligent Search is similar to a company's search for the correct candidate in that both are defined as much by the order of the search as it is by the actual steps involved. I've repeatedly heard very smart people tell me that they started their search by calling a few agencies. I won't make many friends in the agency world by saying this but that should be the last step in your job search, one that only comes after you've exhausted your own resources. The reasons that people give for calling agencies first are usually things like, "I'm too busy to do all that work myself" or "I know they have opportunities that I don't have access to on my own" or very simply, "She's really nice and she helped me find my current job."

Having spent one third of my recruiting career making a very good living in the agency world, 95% of what I was doing, the candidate could easily have done for themselves. Over and over I would place someone in a job at a company that they drove past every day but never stopped to ask if it might be worth dropping off a resume. But before we even get to that step it is important to understand yourself and your own personal situation.

The first criteria in the course of your job search should be to have a clear vision of your personal sense of urgency in finding a new position. If you've just been laid off or terminated and need income as quickly as possible to pay your bills, you are in a much different situation than someone who is receiving a paycheck and only considering a job change if the perfect situation arises.

Tom was just informed by his manager that due to an economic slowdown his position had been eliminated and other than a two-week severance, Tom had no other income. "I was devastated. I had started in this company just six months prior, knew that I was doing a good job, and shame on me, had no clue that we were in severe financial straits. I had no vacation time accrued, and was literally looking at the possibility that I wouldn't be able to pay my rent the next month unless I found something immediately."

These "surprise attacks" require immediate action on your part but in no way change the order of events that should occur. What someone in Tom's position must do is move more quickly than someone with the luxury of time on his side and focus his full attention on finding his next job. Tom may not have the opportunity to consider his long-term goals on a job change since the short-term goal of finding something fast takes priority. Tom's situation is unfortunate but he needs to recognize a few realities. One of those is that he can't afford to be too choosy. Another is that he may not have the luxury of negotiating any details of his offer. While Tom's situation is unfortunate, it would be more unfortunate if he lost the first opportunities to come his way because he was holding out for a salary equal or better than his most recent position.

For Mary, considering a job change is a much different matter. While she is still relatively happy in her current situation, it is becoming obvious to her that she will never reach her long-term goals in her current company. She knows she needs to start exploring other avenues and also knows she

can take her time finding exactly the right
scenario for herself.

For both of these candidates, however, the first few
steps remain the same: create a clear definition of your next
position, write your resume, and start making personal
contacts.

Chapter 13, Define Your Desired Position

Evaluate What You Want: Regardless of the urgency of your search, three steps define an Intelligent Search. An astounding number of people head out the door to an interview without really knowing what it is they want. The first thing any agency will do for you which you can and should do for yourself more than once in your career, is figure out what you don't like about your current job and what you'd like to find in your next position. Guess what? *You'll never know if you found the right position if you have not defined what you want.*

The results of this self-analysis are as varied as the people looking for jobs. The list of items that any candidate wants is both tangible and intangible. The tangibles are those that are easy to define and easy to see when you find them. They include things like:

- Proximity to your home
- A window office

- Work from home
- An office vs. cubicle

- $4,000 more in salary
- Stock options

- Pension fund
- Laptop computer

- 3 weeks of vacation
- Casual work clothes

- Title of manager
- Travel opportunity

Over the course of the interview process, and sometimes even before the interview, through a company website, this information is all verifiable. But the intangible list of "wants" can be much harder to assess and very easy for any company to claim, yet you can't prove them until you are in the experience. They include things like:

- Entrepreneurial environment

- Pleasant work atmosphere

- Recognize and reward achievement

- Team spirit

- High energy people

- Strong leadership

- Company ethics

- Smart people

- Commitment to excellence

- 9-5 hours

As important as these items might be, even the most savvy shopper can be fooled about the nature of these issues until actually on board. It is still important however to define both your ideal environment and your ideal position, recognizing that there is compromise in any major decision. Once you've defined this list for yourself, keep it somewhere close at hand and use it as a measure throughout your career search.

Write Your Resume: The next step is to put together a resume that will get you in the door for an interview. If you could get the interview without a resume, there would be no reason to have one but since getting the interview is going to require a resume in 99% of the cases, you have little choice. There are many excellent books on resume writing and I have no intention of covering that material in this book, but I do have one important piece of advice from the perspective of the person reading your resume. Somehow the notion has become popular that no resume should be more than one page. Any experienced recruiter will tell you that while one page works when you only have two years of experience, it tells almost nothing when you have over five years of experience. Amazingly enough, I see resumes on a regular basis, of candidates with 20 years of experience, who still carry a one-page resume. If the resume book you are using as a reference suggests that all resumes should be one page, buy a different book.

Some of the most common resume mistakes that recruiters see besides the one pager, is the tendency to try to hide entire jobs, dates of degrees, implied degrees that were never completed, generic resumes with no chronology or history, and the all too common cute resume, as in "wouldn't it be cute if I turned the page sideways to get attention." The cute resume gets the wrong kind of attention and special fonts often are not scannable by companies using resume scanners. Special backgrounds, special paper, and photographs of yourself are not endearing you to any recruiter either. In the advertising or marketing world, those little tricks may be more appreciated, but to the average recruiter, they are just a turn-off.

Evaluate Your Market: Once you've defined your ideal position and written your resume, there is only one more important piece of your preparation. *Study your job market!*

More potential jobs are lost or turned down over a lack of current information regarding the local job market than any other reason. One of the quickest ways to gauge your job market is to pick up a Sunday paper and see in a broad sense what the "hot spots" are for your local areas. If there are very few jobs advertised for architects or engineers, that is probably a pretty accurate indicator of your market. This does not mean you should stop looking but it does mean you must be reasonable in what you expect to find. The other clear way to check the temperature of your job market is to talk to people in your particular field and geographical consideration. If someone at your local radio station tells you they receive 300 resumes for every position, be prepared for an uphill climb.

> *A fellow recruiter once told me, "We thought we had found the perfect candidate. We had reviewed at least a hundred resumes, interviewed ten candidates, and narrowed it down to this one. Who would have thought that she would quote an expected salary $10,000 more than we needed or were ready to pay? Her salary quote was higher than candidates with twice her experience. I ran into her months later after we had hired another candidate and I asked her where she had gotten the idea of the salary she quoted and she said she had a friend in New York City in a similar job and that's what he suggested she should expect. Her friend knew nothing about the job market in Akron, Ohio and nothing about the supply and demand in that area for her specific skills but somehow he felt confident offering her advice...that is, assuming he was even honest with her about what he was making!"*

Now that you've completed the first three steps of an Intelligent Search, 1) define your goal, 2) write your resume, and 3) know your market, you're ready to start the search.

Chapter 14, Networking and the Internet

Using your own internal network effectively is really the heart of any Intelligent Search. Sit down with pen and paper or at your computer and really think. You are about to do the most difficult piece of the job, but possibly the most valuable. It will be the most important element of a successful search.

Start organizing your thoughts by first listing all the companies that are in a business that is competitive or related to your current or most recent company. For example, if you are currently in a pharmaceutical company, list all the other local pharmaceutical firms. There are plenty of lists out there that can make this step easier. One of my favorites is the Book of Business Lists published by the Business Journal. These books which are very large, magazine-format compendiums can be found in any major book store and are updated on a regular basis.

Next begin to list all the businesses that peripherally support those businesses. Again there are several resources to use for this including many trade publications. This list may include large consulting firms, major software vendors with products that are used by that industry, or in some cases third-party providers to those businesses.

Once your lists of companies are complete, start a third list. This list will include all the people you can possibly think of with whom you've worked in the past or present. Using this internal network is integral to your success. Think about people of whom you thought highly in your last couple of jobs. List them. Consider people you've met through trade shows or business conferences and list them. Again, it is important to be as thorough as possible at this point. If you carry a Rolodex or business card scanner, it can help prompt your memory.

Start a fourth list. On this list you'll include people who may be relatives, neighbors, old college friends, team members from your local gym, and people with whom you've socialized over the year. If you review people you may have met through holiday parties or summer barbecues the list can really grow.

These four lists become your search stepping-stones. Your most likely entrée into your next position is *through someone you already know*. When you embark on a job search it is important to be thorough and organized and your four lists will help you conduct an Intelligent Search. Go back to list number one and ask yourself if you know someone in that company and write their name next to the company name. Continue on through your first two lists doing this same exercise. Again, any reliance on business cards or past training sessions could be helpful.

Next, put together a clean, concise script that you will use to introduce yourself to these people and let them know you are actively conducting a job search, or exploring new opportunities. Ask them if they can get a copy of your resume to the appropriate people. Even though you can do this yourself through most company web sites, your chances of being given serious consideration are greater if you are being introduced through an employee referral program. Your script may say something like the following:

> *"Hi Joe, I don't know if you remember me but we met at a recent conference and I was impressed with our discussion. I'm exploring new opportunities and wondered if you could pass my resume to the appropriate person for consideration in your organization?"*

There is no need on these initial calls to do more than the most cursory introduction of yourself. In most cases, people are more than happy to help especially if their company has implemented an aggressive employee referral program. Be polite and courteous and call through your four lists of companies and contacts. In some cases the person may direct you to their company website and assure them that you also intend to do that but you were hoping they could be instrumental in having it brought personally to the attention of the appropriate parties. If they tell you their company is not currently hiring ask them if they have heard of any that are. For example, where did the last person who left their company go? This extra prompting often opens up significant leads for your search.

At this point, many of you may be thinking, "Wow, this is a lot of work. Why don't I just call an agency to do all of this for me?" There are times when using an agency is very effective but there are multiple reasons not to use them as your first course of action and that will be further discussed in Chapter 16.

I won't say "Don't get discouraged." When you are looking for a job, it does get discouraging if you are not getting any response. Most companies no longer acknowledge the receipt of your resume. But trust that you've completed the most difficult part of any job search and you haven't even resorted to any of the more commonplace options for finding a job.

The second most successful avenue for finding a new job is *the Internet*. The Internet is a goldmine of opportunities and is becoming more and more attractive as it continues to mature. For many professionals in non-computer related jobs, the Internet is as much a mystery as is the entire world of computer technology, but it is extremely important that you not overlook its usefulness in a career search. If you can't navigate the "information superhighway" on your own, *ask for help*. Someone you know is extremely fluent in Internet technology and can show you what you need to do. I recommend a book called "America's Top Internet Job Sites" as a very good primer on the Internet Job Highway.

In Chapter 4, we provided a list of many of the most common Internet job sites. The one that is leading the way is Monster.com. During a strong economy, it is not at all unusual for someone to post their resume on Monster.com and receive 10-20 calls within the first few days. However, here are some tips that can help you when you are working in any of these Internet sites:

- First of all, the receiving company gets your resume in a format that is very difficult to read. Offer to send them a clean copy as soon as you are contacted.

- Leave the salary question open or at your current salary. Many times candidates are "whimsical" and put in a very high number wondering if they will get any calls. Unfortunately many companies do not call based on the salary requested because it is well over their position requirements. More importantly, your resume is now in their database for all future reference *with the salary as quoted*, possibly losing you many interviewing opportunities.

- Be sure that your contact information is correct. A surprising number of typos are made in telephone numbers and e-mail addresses.

- Allow plenty of room on your answering machine or voice-mail service for the possibility of many responses to your resume. It's a good idea to change any cute or musical voice-mail messages during a job search to a more professional or neutral message.

- Be prepared to respond to all the companies that contact you. Again, information like "no call back" can sit in a company database for years and reflect poorly on your character.
- At least initially, weed out any companies that are agencies offering to help in your job search. Politely let them know you are in preliminary stages and not prepared to use any outside services at this stage but you'll save their contact information for future use.
- *Most importantly, understand that if your own company is using the Internet, they may see your resume and recognize you by your experience, even if you've left the name field confidential.* Be prepared ahead of time how to handle this possibility and know what to expect of their reactions.

We can all expect the use of the Internet to continue to substantially expand in the next few years. It is no surprise that its impact in the technology and specialty sectors is already extremely visible, but it seems obvious that it will continue to grow beyond these sectors in the very near future. There are specific sites for administrative positions, architects, sales positions, executives, customer service positions, and more. As it continues to grow there will be more and more specialized sites until eventually it will be the most common method for a job search.

The Internet can be especially helpful for a candidate who is considering multiple geographic portions of the country. However, job seekers should be very honest with themselves when considering relocation. *Statistically, other than in the very early years of a career, a permanent relocation is unsuccessful unless the candidate already has family ties or friends in the region to which they are moving.*

In many companies over 50% of their hiring is through a combination of employee referrals and the Internet. Using these two methods of job searching successfully can get you more than halfway home in your own search. In our next chapter, we will explore more traditional avenues of a job search.

Chapter 15, More Job Search Alternatives

We've now established that your most effective methods of a job search are your own networking and the Internet, but there are other avenues that you can pursue in parallel during your search. The oldest method, and one that used to hold an exclusive place in a job search is your local newspaper classifieds. The biggest mistake I see candidates make when looking through the classifieds is assuming that unless they see their specific qualifications mentioned, the company does not need their skills and they should not bother to send a resume. Newspaper advertising is expensive. It is difficult to place an ad that lists every position a company may be trying to fill at any particular time, so if you see a company that might meet your carefully defined requirements, consider sending a resume. There are a few rules of thumb to follow in responding to print advertising:

- *First and most obvious*, look for specific mention of your skills and respond to those ads. After sending your resume, it's worth following up on these opportunities with a phone call after a week or two, especially if you know you have the exact work experience being requested in the ad. However, many times companies who hire regularly run what are referred to as "laundry list" ads. They may not have a specific need for that skill today, but because they hire it on a relatively frequent basis, it gets thrown into the ad as a catch all and to build a resume database for future reference. One call is sufficient to bring attention to the resume you sent. If you receive no call back, let it go.

Repeated calls only annoy the company representative and bring attention to you in all the wrong ways.

- *Second, send a resume to any company running an extremely large ad.* A company running quarter page and half page ads is probably doing extensive hiring at all levels. In most cases companies do not run ads for entry level positions or even mention entry level opportunities in the ads they run but if you are looking for an entry level position it won't hurt to send a resume to companies running large ads. If you are an entry level candidate, I suggest that you do *not* follow up these particular resumes with a phone call. These calls are annoying to the company and a waste of your time regardless of what you may have been told. There are other more effective ways to use that same time.

- *Third, while you are browsing the classifieds* get a red pen or crayon and circle how many times you see your skill set reflected. If this exercise results in only one or two circles, recognize that no matter how good you are at what you do, the demand for your particular skill in your home town is probably very small. It might be wise to check the Internet to be sure that the situation is represented equally. The fact that there is little demand for your skill hopefully warns you that any job change may be a difficult one for you and helps set your expectations. This fact also sets a different tone to any offer negotiation, and hopefully points out for you the need to expand your experience. On the other hand, if you see pages full of red circles after this exercise, you know that you will very definitely find a position and you just need to be diligent in knowing what is important to you in choosing a job where you will be happy and rewarded.

- *Finally*, recognize that sending a resume to a company when you see positions you'd like to have but for which you have no experience, is not a fruitful use of your time. Your best chance of getting a position you want where you have either no experience or only academic experience is through your own network or your school connections.

Job Fairs: Another excellent option in your job search is to use local job fairs. Job fairs have gotten an undeserved bad rap over the years particularly from the perspective of senior professionals who often believe they are a waste of time. Many job fairs cater specifically to a particular field or industry such as technical or sales professionals. From the employers' viewpoint I have found job fairs to be a very fertile hunting ground when they are well run and well publicized. For a candidate who may have minimal experience but great presentation and communication skills they are a must. Even in a five-minute introduction, a company that finds a candidate who presents well will make the effort to scour the resume more closely for any kind of a fit within their organization.

Occasionally you will see a job fair advertised with only one company in attendance. This is basically an open house but is conducted off-site at a hotel or conference center. This is more common if the company is headquartered out of town or has a facility that is not conducive to candidate attendance either aesthetically or geographically.

Do not go to a job fair expecting to walk away with an offer, although there are companies that will take the process that far in exceptional cases. Attend the job fair

93

expecting to spend five minutes with each company representative unless they invite you to interview on the spot. Here are a few tips to keep in mind while attending job fairs:

- Dress professionally. Regardless of how relaxed the job fair environment may be, it is still your first impression. Make a good one.

- Be organized as you tour the job fair. *Read the catalogue provided.* Understand that each company representative is shaking hands and greeting candidates all day. Candidates who ask "What does your company do?" are an immediate turnoff since they are provided with material ahead of time that answers those questions.

- Don't eat or drink while you are speaking with reps regardless of how many treats are being provided. Job fairs tend to offer many food items to attract candidates to the booth, but eating popcorn as you try to discuss your experience is not the best reflection on you.

- If you don't have a firm, dry handshake simply don't shake hands at all. If you know you are nervous and that is causing wet hands, carry your resume in your arms in a way that prevents you easily being able to shake hands. Under those circumstances, not shaking hands is excusable.

- Bring plenty of resumes and have them easily accessible so you don't need to scrounge through a briefcase at every booth. For large job fairs, it is likely that there will be over 100 companies. Be prepared.

- When a company representative tells you they do not have jobs that meet your qualifications, *don't argue with them.* No matter how desperate your situation may be, telling a company that they have overlooked your value to their organization is not the way to get an interview.

- Understand that sometimes companies man the job fair booth with managers or other company representatives. Do not assume you are talking with HR or a recruiter when you may be speaking directly with a hiring manager or future peer. It is appropriate to ask the person's role within the organization if they have not provided a business card that is self-explanatory.

- Don't monopolize the time of any representative unless they are freely offering it. Many companies are there for a cursory assessment of you and to collect resumes.

- Be alert and make careful observations. If the company representatives look bored, unenthusiastic, or disrespectful of you it may be an important indication about their organization. Mark down notes that will help you remember your impressions later.

- If you know someone at the organization, be sure to mention it! It may help you get an interview when the person is well thought of and speaks favorably of you. Make sure you've already contacted this person and forwarded a resume to them so they can claim any existing employee referral fees and act as a reference on your behalf.

All of the tips above also apply to attendance at any open house. An open house differs from a job fair in that you are only meeting with one specific company at a company site. Open houses are almost always manned with hiring managers as well as HR and recruiters. An open house is a great way to see the actual facilities and get more information about a company's culture. In attending an open house, you are very definitely expected to know what the company does so go prepared with information you've gathered through the Internet or any other source.

Many open houses are by invitation only and are on a scheduled basis. Be on time as there may be group sessions and tours that you must attend. You may learn of open houses through your local classifieds, through radio or TV advertising, or from a friend. Take advantage of this opportunity to explore the facility as well as meet company representatives.

Open houses are run differently at each company. Some are meant as a way to conduct formal interviews, but many are just an introduction to the company and an initial screening process for candidates with the intention of inviting selected candidates back for the full interview process. When attending an open house act as a "guest" on your best behavior. Feel free to ask questions and be prepared to leave with enough impressions to make a judgment as to whether you would want to work there or not.

Outplacement Services: If your job search is a consequence of having been laid off from your current employer, you may be offered the possibility of outplacement services. While many people are disinclined to take advantage of this service especially when they are angry or upset with their separation from the company, it is a good idea to take them up on the offer.

Outplacement services are not intended to find you a job. They are a resource to use at the outset of your job search. They are meant to help you through the emotional roller coaster of having been let go and to get you focused on finding a new job. Outplacement is paid for by your previous employer, and from the company perspective, is a tool to minimize potential litigation and help you through a difficult time. The quality of these services varies tremendously but anyone going in with the intention of gaining something from the experience will definitely benefit from some part of the programs offered.

Many outplacement services offer online sites where local hiring companies advertise their own needs so at the very least, be sure to access their web site for posted opportunities.

If you are entry level or in a career transition, your college or trade school most likely offers on-campus interview opportunities. Be sure to attend as many of these as possible. Some of these are structured so multiple companies are in attendance at one time. Others may be individual, visiting companies. The attraction of these events is that you know immediately that the company is hiring entry level or they would not have taken the time and expense to attend.

Keep in mind that although being in your school environment may breed a sense of comfort on your part, this is still a first impression scenario and you must project your best image. Many times the information captured by a company may be saved in a resume database for all eternity. As in any job search method you use, be sure that they will have saved a positive impression of you.

Chapter 16, Agencies and Retained Search

Perhaps in reading the last two chapters, you've asked yourself, "Why wouldn't I just pick up the phone, call a few agencies and let them do all this work for me? After all, it doesn't cost me anything, right?" Wrong!

The fact that you don't pull money out of your pocket to pay them does not mean it is a free service to you. Your payment is less direct but very real and can mean a great deal of money out of pocket during salary negotiations. Think about it. You want a job with Company A. They have two candidates in consideration, you being one of them. They come to decision time and Candidate A came to them through an employee referral or Internet posting. You came in through an agency. Right up front, you are going to cost the company a great deal of money, easily over $15,000 in the technical world. Generally there is a 30-day guarantee and after that they've lost it should either of you decide it's not working out. This plays a significant part in the decision-making and may be the reason you never get the offer.

In the same scenario, if you have a little less of what is needed for the position than the other candidate, but they like you more, they still have to decide if it is worth hiring you with the fee attached. Having been the hiring company I can tell you that many times I wished the candidate had come to us directly because we would have made an offer if it weren't for the fee. Taking a chance on a candidate without all the skills is a judgment call. It becomes harder to justify taking a chance when the company must absorb the agency fee if it doesn't work out.

On the other hand, let's say you are the best candidate and the company decides to pay the fee and extend an offer.

Let's say their offer is just a couple thousand lower than what you were hoping. It's tough to find room to pay you either more salary or some sort of a sign-on bonus when the agency fee is part of the package. Without the agency fee there is generally a little more flexibility on your package.

Now that you understand that going directly to an agency *before using more direct resources* can significantly impact your likelihood of getting an offer or negotiating your compensation, there are even more important issues to consider. Some of the unseemly stories you've perhaps heard about the world of headhunters and agencies are probably true. Consider for example that you've sent your resume to an agency. Of course, you've given them all sorts of stipulations like "don't send it anywhere unless you talk to me first." There is not an agency in the world that can be successful under those types of guidelines. They know that whatever other resources you are using, they must beat you to the punch otherwise they will not be first in the door. The world of the Internet makes this even more of a concern as they know they are trying to get your resume to the company before the company pulls it off the Internet for themselves.

Where the resume came from first has lost more candidates interviews than you can ever imagine. The agent, who you believe is working on your behalf, has no problem losing the interview for you if they think they will not receive a fee. It is not unusual for an agency to misrepresent what they know about a candidate if they feel the company may hire around them to avoid their fee. It is also not unheard of to tell you untrue stories about the company who wants to interview you because if you take a job you found yourself, the agency has no chance of placing you. Sounds pretty unscrupulous but it happens quite often. All that said, is there ever a time when you should use an agency in your job search? Yes.

If you have exhausted your own resources and spent a couple months following all the ideas outlined in an Intelligent Search, you have nothing to lose by going to an agency. An agency is going to follow the same steps that you have hopefully already done on your own. They will send your resume to the major competitors of whatever company you were at most recently. You should already have done that step. They will match your skills against other companies that have advertised for similar skills in the classifieds. You should already have done that step, also. They will match your resume with whatever company postings they can find on the Internet which you will have already done.

So, where can an agency add value? They can get your resume to some of the smaller companies of which you may never have heard because they don't spend much on advertising. They can "talk you up" to any manager with whom they have had contact and possibly get you an interview when your resume alone was unsuccessful. If they get you an interview, they can generally share some insights regarding what to expect in your interview process and some inside information on a particular manager. If you are relocating to another city, they can connect with other agencies in those cities to aid in your job hunt. These are all helpful in your search.

The following guidelines in choosing and working with agencies will make a difference in how successful they can be on your behalf:

- *Use one agency at a time*. Work with one and if you are unhappy with their progress, let them know they no longer represent you and to stop any efforts on your behalf.
- *Find one that specializes in your field*. While not every industry has agencies that specialize there are many that do including sales,

technical, nursing, healthcare, and manufacturing.

- *Meet the agency contact in person.* Never work with an agency when you haven't met your contact. This person is going to represent you and if they come across as ruthless or unethical, it will reflect on you. Also, if they have met you they are more able to accurately describe you to a hiring manager. Having made that rule, understand that even when you have met the person, they may be doing "splits" with dozens of other agencies that you've never met. For example, they may have your resume but another agency has a company where you are a fit. They will get your resume into the right hands and "split" whatever fee they earn.

- *Use your judgment.* First and foremost, agency employees are trying to make a living. Looking out for your interests is at best, their second priority. Find one you can trust.

- *Get feedback on interviews.* Many times the agency is equally frustrated by lack of feedback from a manager after an interview. Often, however, they have gotten a "no" and never bothered to fill you in. In most cases a good agent will call you within 24 hours to get your feedback and also relay any feedback they may have gotten on you.

- *Don't allow them to misrepresent your experience.* It is common for an agency to tailor your resume to get you into an interview. The company will realize this as soon as you are in the interview process and will wonder if it was your misrepresentation or the agency. Don't let an agency change dates or alter the experience on your resume.

101

- *Make your own decisions.* After getting an offer from a company through an agency, you may feel a lot of pressure to accept the position. Be prepared to ask for a little time to make certain of your decision. You either want it or you don't. Don't be swayed.

- *Be respectful.* Agency work is hard work especially when you find a good agent. Like real estate it is a commission-based pay scale. It takes years of experience to be good at the job and a strong character to do it ethically. Too often people perceive that headhunters make a lot of money for doing very little. In reality, if you are using a reputable agent, they have years of experience and know the hiring market amazingly well. Due to their large network, they can spread word about you faster than you can ever believe. Make sure what they spread is good news.

Using an agency for any entry-level position is not a realistic strategy. Using agencies when you are trying to make a career transition, meaning you have no work experience in the field into which you are trying to enter, does you a disservice. Companies pay fees for experienced people. An inexperienced person they can find at no cost. An agency should tell you that they cannot help you without at least one year of experience in that field but will sometimes "take a chance" that they can get you in the door with less. This is a disservice to you as you may get an interview directly but not with a fee involved.

Retained Search Firms: A retained search firm is an executive recruiting company that *finds you* for a hiring company instead of vice-versa. They are paid, partially in advance, with the remainder of the fee paid as the search progresses. *How can you tell whether you're talking to an agency or a retained search firm?* An executive recruiter conducting a retained search will tell you all about the company and the position up front because they are earning a retained fee without trying to compete with other services. Agencies, on the other hand, are reluctant to share information with you about a particular company position because they don't want you to go there directly or tell another agency. Furthermore, retained search is generally for positions with salaries over six figures.

In the world of retained search, there is big money at stake in finding the right person. If a company tells you they do "both retained and contingent," it means they may have done one or two retained searches ever but more likely do all contingent but *would like* to be able to get a retained fee search.

If you are a senior level executive, I would advise that you always take or return calls from the retained search world. Most senior level executives will make career changes through this network. Most retained search is nationwide. If you receive a call from an executive recruiter in the retained search world, they have identified which companies and which candidates within those companies to pursue. Take advantage of these calls to find out more about how your qualifications match up against the requirements and what sort of compensation package is involved. There are too many good retained search companies to name them all but if you are interested in knowing their names, there are directories available that list most of the major ones such as Spencer Stuart, Korn/Ferry, Heidrick and Struggles, and dozens more.

If you are conducting a senior level search you should look up the web sites of some of these services and submit a resume or scan their list of opportunities available.

As you can see, in conducting an Intelligent Search, you are taking responsibility for the same exercises that an agency will do for you. It takes more effort on your part but is more gratifying and financially rewarding in the long run.

Chapter 17, Interviews and Offers

Before getting to specific advice on interviewing and offer negotiation, let me point out one fact that you must understand while sending out resumes and using your network. *The fact that your friend or brother didn't like a particular company does not mean it isn't the right place for you at a specific time in your career.* Chances are that you and your best friend are not going to choose the same spouse or buy the same house. While taking some advice from your friends is smart, the ultimate decision making must be yours and it needs to happen based on your interview process. I've seen too many candidates turn down interviews because their friend didn't have a positive experience. Your career may need exactly what this position has to offer. Furthermore, large organizations differ tremendously from one department to another. Respect the advice of your friends, but think for yourself. All you lose by going on an interview is a few hours. Many times those who interview you will move on and remember you—hopefully with positive impressions—from the interview process. One final reason to take advantage of any interview is simply for more experience at being interviewed; just like anything else, practice makes perfect.

Okay, so let's assume you've earned an interview—and *earned* is exactly correct if you've conducted an Intelligent Search—through your own resources. What can you expect during the interview process?

Each company conducts interviews in its own way so the first rule of thumb is to *be ready for anything.* During the phone call that schedules the interview with you, ask what to expect in terms of time spent in the interview process. Ask how many people you will be meeting. Then be prepared to have all of that thrown right out the window once you arrive.

The interview process is like a first date. Both sides want to make the best first impression. Taking careful directions so you can be on time, dressing well, and treating everyone you meet with respect is critical. Your interview starts with the first person you meet which in many cases may be the receptionist. You may be asked to fill out an application. While this exercise seems a repetition of what is on your resume, be aware that an application is a legal document and you are giving a company the authorization to confirm anything you write down. Not only can you lose an offer by misrepresenting any information, but it is also cause for immediate dismissal should you be hired and begin your new job.

Once you've reached the interview stage, leaving your salary information blank is a waste of time. Eventually you must provide that data and the application is the place to accurately record this information. Some people tell me they don't want to put down their salary information because they want a "fair" offer and not an offer based solely on their current salary. I understand this rationale but the fact of the matter is, a company still has the right to request this information. If it is not captured on the application, it can lead to many hours invested on your part in the interview process with an un-negotiable compensation issue at the end of all your time invested. Besides, in truth, you don't know what a "fair" offer is for this particular company or for the responsibilities of the position because you haven't learned enough yet.

Once the application is completed, you should take the opportunity to watch the people you see coming and going in the lobby. Do they look happy? Do you hear laughter in the halls? Are people passing concerned about whether you need a drink, need to hang up your coat, are waiting too long? These are all important clues about the company of which you will want to take note.

One of the biggest mistakes I see candidates make in the interview process is to assume that you are the one being interviewed. Remember the first date scenario? Both of you need to walk away fully informed as to whether you'd like to see each other again. The company doesn't want to show you all their warts and bad habits any more than you want to reveal yours. On your first date, if you start by telling your companion all your worst faults, chances are there will be no second date. You have faults. The company has faults. Your job throughout the interview process is to gather both directly and subtly the information that will help you determine your own interest in proceeding. Be assured that the company is picking up their own set of visible and invisible signals from you during the interviews.

Frequently the next step after filling out the application will be to meet with HR or a recruiter. This person may be collecting basic information regarding your job history and accomplishments or they may be taking more in-depth information as an initial screening. If a company tells you to expect to meet three or four people and, after meeting with one, closes the interview process, something has probably gone wrong; in a most polite way, ask what it might be. For example, "I was told to expect to meet three or four people today, and I'm assuming by closing the interview, there is some information I've provided that changes that scenario. Can you please help me by explaining what that might be?" While you may feel this is a bold question, it's really not at all, and I guarantee if you don't ask it now, you'll never find out. Once you've walked out the door of any interview your chances of some honest feedback are small. You may or may not get a direct response but at least you will have tried. Obviously if you were rude to anyone or poorly dressed, you may be able to answer your own question.

Let's assume you are then introduced to the next person in the interview process. Here are some hard and fast rules to follow with each person:

- Do not assume they have had time to closely scrutinize your resume. Unfortunately many interviews take place around hundreds of other activities in the course of the day and often the interviewer is not as prepared as you should be before the interview.

- As you are moved around, ask each person directly what their role is, where they fit in the organization, and how long they've been there. If you don't have a clear picture in your head, you are likely to go off in all the wrong directions with your answers. Also, unless it is a relatively new company, meeting four people, all of whom have been with the organization less than a year or so, is a red flag to consider later.

- Ask each person what they feel are the most important aspects of the position you are pursuing. Once you know what they feel is important to the job, explain exactly what you've done along similar lines even if it is already on your resume. You may say something like, "If you look at page two on my resume, you'll see that is very much what I did at ABC company." Then elaborate.

- Let each person know what it is about the position that sounds exciting to you and why you are interested.

- Act enthusiastic about the responsibilities. Hopefully you are already enthusiastic but if not, let them know what parts do sound attractive.

- *Never, ever, ever* say anything negative about your prior company, manager, or co-workers. Regardless of how many times I've given this advice it still loses many a candidate the chance at an offer because they can't stop themselves from putting down their past employers. There are other ways to get your point across without denigrating your past company. Besides, most recruiters who have been around a few years have already heard the horror stories from neighboring companies.

- In case it's not obvious, do *not* ask questions such as "How many hours would I be expected to work?" or "How long do I need to stay in this position before I get out of it?" They will reflect poorly on your work ethic. While you may need this information to make your final decision, these type questions are best asked once an offer is on the table and should be phrased in a positive manner. Specific benefit questions are also best asked once an offer has been extended. Many times full benefits details are listed on a company website.

- Do feel free to ask why the position is open. Where did the last person go who held this position? How long were they in the role? These kinds of questions will get you the information you want in a much more positive way.

- End each interview by asking what you can expect in the next step. Ask them how your background compares with other candidates they have met for this position. Ask if there is anyone internally being considered for this role. All of this information is relatively easy to ask while you are there but almost impossible to find out once you leave. Ask when you can realistically expect a decision and whom should you call for follow-up.

- Being relaxed during the interviews is a good thing but don't get so relaxed that you let yourself use sloppy or offensive language.
- Be wary of offers made on the spot. While it may be flattering, it may also be a red flag that the company is somewhat desperate to fill the position. Let them know you are flattered but will need time to assess your best career option.

Now you've completed your interviews, sometimes over the course of one day, sometimes taking two or three visits. Waiting to hear a decision from a company is extremely frustrating. If you asked as you left the interview when you can expect to hear back, you have a guideline as to when you should call to follow up. Wait a day or two after the decision point that you've been told, and then call your primary contact and ask if a decision has been made. Be sure to let them know that you are very interested. If you are time-pressured because you have other offer considerations, let them know your time constraints.

If you felt the interviews went well but you were not extended an offer, one phone call can answer your questions. Very politely ask the person with whom you felt most comfortable to please help you out by providing specific information as to why you are not the best fit for the job. Don't argue with what they tell you but take advantage of their hospitality to highlight experience that may not have been clearly communicated in the interview process. I would personally prefer to see this information supplied in a follow-up letter but feel that any candidate deserves an honest answer as to why they were not chosen. You've invested your time and it will help you to know what you may have done wrong in the interview process. If the answer is that you are not as close a cultural fit as another candidate, you have nothing to do but accept that decision. However, if it is a salary issue or something you miscommunicated in the interview process, this may be your only chance to clarify your situation or experience.

It is not unusual, especially in large corporations, for offer decisions to take months. If you are in a position to allow for this time frame it is not an issue. But when you are out of work and need to accept a position, it is extremely frustrating. Keep it in perspective. If the timing doesn't work, you still learned a lot about the company and if you left on a positive note, you may be kept in consideration for future positions.

One of the most discouraging parts of a recruiter's job is to tell a candidate who was well-liked that they didn't get the job. When there is hard news to deliver, it sometimes gets put off for weeks and weeks. If your phone call is not returned within a few days, let it go. In most likelihood, you are not getting an offer and you need to focus on the next interview process.

Many times we are so excited that the search and interview process is over that we forget to carefully evaluate what we experienced there. This is even more common when we are anxious to leave our current company and position or when we are out of work and need a job. Take the time to mentally review your interviews, and consider the following important points:

- A company that has a hard time making a decision is telling you something about the culture of its workplace. If that is not your style, take this as a warning; you may be as frustrated working there as you were in the interview process.
- When an interviewer answers the phones or responds to E-mails while you are in their office for an interview, it should tell you

something about them. Pay attention but don't judge the whole company by their behavior.

- How organized was your interview process? Were you kept informed as to what to expect next? How politely were you treated? Did you leave excited or feeling just *so-so*? Did the company make you feel special or part of a cattle call?

- Did the job itself interest you? Did it offer you a challenge beyond your current experience level?

- Do you want to work at this company in this position?

Negotiating an Offer: Once you've decided that you are definitely interested, you are ready to entertain any offers that may be extended. Having an offer extended to you is tricky business. Chances are you'll want to negotiate at least a part of the offer package. Here are some rules for negotiating:

- *Rule Number 1* on receiving a verbal offer is to immediately let them know that you are excited and appreciative of the offer. Regardless of whether that is the case, your first sentence should be "I was very excited throughout the interview process and am pleased to be receiving a formal offer." While you may now have a verbal offer in hand, no offer is considered a formal offer until you have it in writing.

- *Rule Number 2* is to be sure you understand all terms of the offer before attempting to negotiate any points. Be prepared to have any questions you may have, answered before you begin to negotiate.

111

- *Rule Number 3* is to negotiate calmly and be sure you know from what you are willing to walk and what you are not. Trying to get a company to change their rules is a waste of your time and theirs. If the policy is "carved in stone" and has never been changed, don't press the point. Sometimes vacation is negotiable, but many times it is not. Sometimes there is some room on salary, sometimes not.

- *Rule Number 4* is that your best chance of getting what you want is to commit to a start date and a definite yes if your needs can be met. For example, telling me that you're not happy with salary, letting me fix it, and then telling me you're unhappy with tuition reimbursement is a piecemeal effort and not a successful negotiating tactic. Instead say "I am excited and ready to start on January 1st if you can increase the salary by $5000 and waive the year-long wait for tuition reimbursement." Be sure about those two or three items because once you've made this statement, going back and asking for more is poor negotiating.

Asking for concessions doesn't mean you'll get them but the company may try to come back with a compromise that is their best effort to meet you halfway. If you are stuck on the salary issue try again, by saying, "Since there is no leeway on the salary issue, can we compensate with either an extra week of vacation or some sort of sign-on bonus?" Give them a chance to fix what they can but don't expect them to move mountains for you.

Remember, you don't know if Candidate B is in the wings and ready to accept whatever they offer. If Candidate B does exist, you can lose yourself the offer by over-negotiating or just being a nuisance. In a successful negotiation, you both give a little.

Asking for a day or two to think about their offer is not unreasonable. Asking for a month or even a couple of weeks can be. If the company is anxious to fill this position and sees you "buying time" while you continue to look around, they would be justified in being concerned. Being offered a position is a little like a marriage proposal. If someone asks "Will you marry me?" getting a reply "I think so but let me date a few more people" isn't exactly heartwarming.

Keep all negotiations friendly by keeping your tone of voice calm but enthusiastic. Once you've reached compromise and resolution, thank them again for all their efforts on your behalf, make a decision, and respond in a timely fashion. Be sure to get the offer you discussed in writing before you resign your position or turn down any other offers.

As one recruiter said, "There have been many candidates I loved during the interview process and grew to hate during offer negotiations." How you negotiate will tell a company a lot about how you handle stressful situations. Be sure what they perceive is positive.

Chapter 18, Summary and Final Thoughts

Change is difficult and changing jobs can be among the most difficult changes in life. Staying in a job that is no longer right for you can be every bit as difficult. When a change is well thought through, it can be the best thing for you and your family. I see candidates on a regular basis who say "I don't know why I stayed there so long." The real reason is that the thought of change was overwhelming and too big a step for them. Hopefully by following the tips in this book, your job change can be less painful. Let's review:

- *Define what you want and don't want in your next job.* Make a list and refer to it as you conduct your job search.

- *Use your own network first.* Be thorough in this step, as it is the most likely source of your next position.

- *Use the Internet aggressively.* The Internet is a powerful tool and getting stronger every day. Use it to your best advantage.

- *Take advantage of job fairs, open houses, outplacement services, and educational and trade school opportunities.* Each of these sources offers its own reward in your job search.

- *Use agencies last.* Even if they are promising you the perfect job, count on the fact that you can find that job yourself and reap a more rewarding compensation package in the long run. When you do turn to an agency for help, use them wisely.

- *Handle the interview process with your best behavior.* You've gotten this far in your job search. Don't ruin it by mishandling the interviews.
- *Negotiate tactfully and successfully.* Know the outcome you desire before beginning negotiation. Don't fall back once a commitment to start at a company is made.

These basic steps will turn any job search into a more organized effort to find the *right* job and the best next step for your career. Let us end by sharing some real life situations.

> *A recruiter told the following story: "I met someone who seemed to be the perfect candidate. He had 25 years of experience, had been in a Big Six accounting firm, owned his own company for a while, answered all of my questions well, interviewed great with all four managers, and we made him a very strong offer which he accepted. As we began checking his references, I was in shock. Nothing, I mean nothing, on his resume was true. He hadn't worked at any of the companies he claimed to have worked, he was not degreed let alone double-degreed as he had claimed, and worse than that, he set up references via E-mail that were all his own E-mail addresses. It was a nightmare. He had already started work and we needed to walk him out of the building. Truly scary."*

Lesson: Don't misrepresent your experience. While you may get away with a lie or two initially, sooner or later, you'll be tripped up. Someone who worked at the same company at the same time you claim to have been there might talk to you about the company and easily realize you were never there. Any type of misrepresentation will cause more trouble down the line and is grounds for termination.

> *"I once represented someone," explained one recruiter, "who got frazzled because he got lost on the way to the interview. He called the company and got directions from the receptionist. When he still couldn't find it, he called again and abused her on the phone. Needless to say they were not interested in interviewing him when he arrived."*

Lesson: Everyone with whom you come in contact while interviewing will remember how you presented yourself, perhaps more so than the words on your resume. Be a professional no matter what happens.

> *One job seeker told me, "At one point in my job search I felt I had found my perfect job. I was really excited and felt the interviews went really well. I was told I was one of two candidates being considered and I was confident I would get an offer. One week later I received the call that they had extended the offer to the other candidate and they had accepted. I told them I was understandably disappointed but wished them the best and asked that they keep me in mind. I was so discouraged. I spent the next few weeks at my current job asking myself what could I have done differently. One day, I walked into my apartment from work and the phone was ringing. I ran to answer it and it was one of the managers to whom I would have reported. She asked if I was still interested. I was. I asked if I needed to come back in again and she said no, she was prepared to*

extend an offer. Turns out the candidate they hired needed to relocate for her spouse and I had made a positive enough impression that they were ready to extend me the offer, which I accepted on the spot."

Lesson: Don't get discouraged and don't overreact. Any interview process is a great chance to network. Making a positive impression can make a difference either in gaining an immediate offer or one further down the road.

One company representative told this story: "We interviewed a woman for a position and we really wanted her to join us. Turns out she was looking for a position as a manager and while we were offering her significant management potential due to growth, she was determined to hold out for a manager title and responsibilities. We called her back a year later and tried again. Still no luck although by then she had moved twice, both times unhappily even though she had gotten the manager role she wanted. Finally, we called her a last time, two full years after her original interview with us. I think we wore her down because this time she accepted our offer. While she did not step in our door as a manager, she was promoted very shortly and within two years was a director with a staff of over 30 professionals."

Lesson: Look at future growth potential as well as immediate reward in any career change. Sometimes the small growing company can offer you more career movement than the large bureaucratic environment.

Pamela Ciccantelli

"I once interviewed at a company," told one candidate, "and it fit most of the list of requirements I had written. But I got to the final interview and the guy doing the interview was so inconsiderate and downright nasty that I decided it wasn't the place for me. HR called me and wanted to know why I was not interested in pursuing their opportunity and I explained that I didn't feel comfortable I could work for a person who was so disrespectful. She had obviously heard this story before and didn't push the issue. When they called me a month later and asked if I was still interested because that manager was no longer with the organization, I jumped at the chance. I felt that the fact that they had taken care of what was obviously a difficult person, reflected positively on the organization as a whole. Someone else might have let that one bad apple spoil the overall impression, but I accepted the offer, started work there, and had a great experience."

Lesson: Use your own judgment. Don't let your own pride or one person cast a shadow over an otherwise positive experience.

A recruiter once told me, "We had a great candidate on the line and we all were excited about getting him on board. He wasn't working at the time which was perfect for us because he could start immediately. When we extended his offer at the number he had quoted at one point during the interview process, he claimed that he would need more than that now that he had looked around a little. We still wanted him and asked what he needed to start with us. First he

118

*wanted more money. When I resolved that issue
with a compromise, he decided he needed a
different title. We resolved that issue and I
thought we were all set. Then he says he needs a
closed office for him to accept. At this point, we
were losing interest and told him at his level we
didn't offer closed offices but hoped he could
overlook that issue. He claimed he had been
shown an office that would be his and he really
felt strongly about it. So we withdrew the verbal
offer. We hadn't put anything in writing because
we wanted to resolve all of his issues first.
Unfortunately he negotiated himself right out of
an offer. We felt we had gone far enough in
meeting his demands."*

Lesson: Don't over negotiate. Know ahead of time what
is important to you and what you can compromise on. Don't
expect a company to meet all of your demands. Let them
know that you will accept if they can resolve an item or two
but be prepared to compromise on your side also. Tell the
company all of your "must haves" in your first counteroffer.
Don't add to your demands.

*"The most frustrating times," said one
recruiter, "are when we are only a thousand or
two apart and neither side will give in. It seems so
silly. After taxes, a thousand dollars is less than
$20 a week. Both sides lose because they won't
compromise. The candidate says what's a
thousand dollars to them and the company says if
he really wants the job he'll come anyway. They
are both wrong. The company may take another
two months to find another candidate. The
candidate could have easily settled for $20 a week*

Pamela Ciccantelli

> *less, proved himself, and financially moved ahead over time. Those are the worst."*

Lesson: Be sure you are evaluating more than salary. Your long term potential with one company could be immeasurably greater over time than your short-term loss. Ask yourself, "Am I gaining experience that makes me more marketable in the future?" If so, it is money in your pocket. Make smart long-term decisions.

Finally, we all get caught up in the rat race. No matter what job you have it is only a job. The important thing is to do work you are proud of but to keep it in perspective with the rest of your life. Nothing any of us do at work will ever be as important as our health, family, and friends. Keeping this larger perspective in mind all through the process will enable you to enjoy the journey more, make better decisions, and succeed in conducting an Intelligent Search.